THAILAND

TIME-LIFE BOOKS/AMSTERDAM

COOKERY AROUND THE WORLD
THAILAND

THIDAVADEE CAMSONG

Food photography: Foodphotography Eising

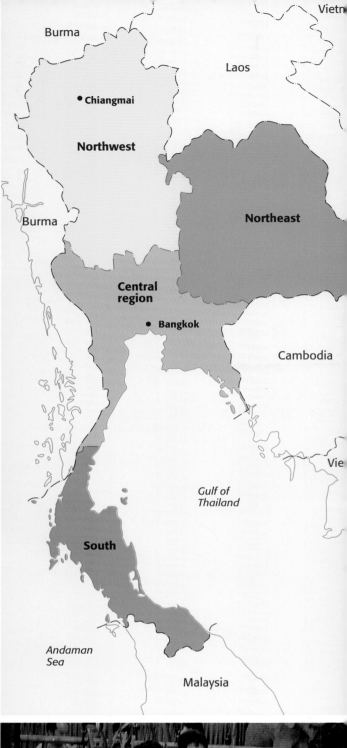

CONTENTS

THAILAND: A TALENT FOR GOOD LIVING

The people of Thailand are epicures: they adore food and they can spend hours talking about what they have just eaten, what they are in the process of eating or what they are going to eat next. Good food is essential to the convivial pleasures of life that the Thais describe

as *sanuk*, roughly meaning "enjoyable" or "good fun", and *sabai*, meaning "comfortable" in the sense of being deliciously full and at ease.

One reason for this happy attitude, as the visitor soon learns, is that the land is a tropical cornucopia of good things to eat. Tempting and exotic foods are on display everywhere in the fertile countryside and villages, and in the towns with their street-corner snack stalls, markets covering almost every space on land or water and wonderful restaurants of all kinds.

Chief among these, and the staple of the Thai diet, is rice—in fact, the Thai invitation to eat, *gin kao*, literally means "eat rice". It grows in brilliant green paddy fields all over the vast central plain and on the sculpted terraces of the mountainous north and west: Thailand is the world's fifth largest producer of rice and the largest exporter. There are many varieties, but the two most important are the long-grain Thai fragrant—or jasmine—rice, fluffy when steamed and served with most savoury dishes, and the high-starch glutinous rice, a sticky short-grain type that forms the basis of many desserts.

A wide choice of foods, herbs and spices go into the dishes that are eaten with the rice. Thai cooks use their abundant fresh seafood—fish, prawns, crabs and mussels—as well as pork, beef, chicken and duck. They make their dishes fiery with chilies and scent them with basil, coriander, shallots, garlic, lemon grass, tamarind, ginger or galangal, and kaffir limes.

Thais grow a range of fruit and vegetables. Perhaps most distinctive and surprising are the exotic nuts and fruits. Farms and orchards provide

coconuts and cashews, as well as exceptionally sweet pineapples, bananas and watermelons, and matchless mangoes, in season from March to May. In addition, there are strawberry-like rambutans, pomelos resembling giant grapefruits, lychees and their smaller cousins, the longans, also known as "dragon's eyes". And, of course, there is the famous durian, so vile smelling that it is not allowed on most ships or aeroplanes but whose creamy flesh is said to taste of ambrosia.

Dozens of cultural strands have woven this varied bounty into a superb cuisine. Home to a Buddhist culture, prizing harmony and balance, Thailand comfortably incorporates earlier Hindu and animist influences. The country is something of a crossroads, with a significant number of Muslims, primarily in the south, and a large Chinese population, as well as historical links to the other nations of Southeast Asia. All of these different influences help to shape Thai cookery.

This book shows you how to cook Thai dishes in your own kitchen. The first chapter introduces you to the country and its people, their regional cuisines and their festivals. Next come six chapters of authentic recipes, with easy-to-follow step-by-step instructions and notes and boxes on some of the more important foods and techniques. The recipes are followed by menu suggestions for both family and more festive meals. Finally, a glossary explains some of the less familiar terms and ingredients used in Thai cuisine.

Taken together, the different sections offer a lively guide to the delights of Thailand and its cookery and a course in simple ways to re-create that cookery at home.

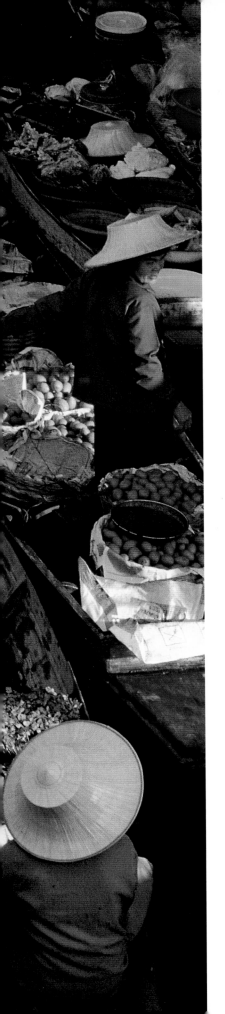

A COUNTRY OF CONTRASTS

Shaped like the head of an elephant, both a Buddhist and a national symbol, beautiful Thailand covers almost 514,000 square kilometres of territory lying at the heart of Southeast Asia. To the north is Laos; the west and northwest border on Burma; the east—the elephant's ear—abuts Cambodia; and the peninsula that forms the elephant's trunk stretches south to Malaysia.

It is a rich landscape, vibrant with colourful and contrasting vegetation. The mountains of the north and northwest, an extension of the Himalayas, are part of the infamous Golden Triangle, home to the opium poppy; but they are also dotted with tea plantations and, on their southern slopes, terraced with rice paddy fields. Rivers descend from these mountains to join others that form the many-branched Chao Phraya, which spreads in a shimmering water system across the country's central flood plain. This is Thailand's green, rice-growing heartland.

Much of the northeast, separated from Laos by the meandering Mekong River, is semi-arid and infertile, with extreme temperatures ranging from over 40°C to freezing. In contrast, the southern peninsula has a tropical rainforest climate and lush vegetation; here are rubber trees and coconut palms, pineapples and cashew nuts.

The coasts border the warm waters of the Andaman Sea and the Gulf of Thailand, which provide abundant catches of fish and crustaceans.

The 56 million people who live in this fortunate land have been moulded by many cultural influences—for example, Indian, Chinese, Malay and Indonesian. They are united, however, by a venerable tradition of nationhood: Thailand has been a major state since the 14th century and unlike the vast majority of its Asian neighbours, it has never been colonized by the West. This unity appears in the people's devotion to their monarchy and to their multi-textured Buddhism (more than 90 per cent of Thais are Buddhist and most young men spend several months of their lives as monks).

Tradition can be sensed in every aspect of Thai life—in the architecture, in the exquisite art and in the delicate kindliness and courtesy that mark Thai behaviour. Within their unity, however, there is room for variety. The Thais are easy-going and adaptable, with a great sense of fun and enormous enthusiasm for the many royal and religous festivals that enliven their year. A convivial people, they enjoy the pleasures of life. This blend of varied cultural influences and a long central tradition, of creative attention and freewheeling enthusiasm, makes their cuisine one of the greatest in the world.

Draped in yellow silk, a sculpted Buddha meditates among the ruins of Sukhothai, the ancient Thai capital. The statue's hand positions call the earth to witness Buddha's merit.

A Long and Proud History

The many-faceted culture that produced Thailand's cuisine has roots that go back thousands of years. As the cave paintings discovered both in the north and south of the country attest, Thailand has been inhabited by artists since the Stone Age and archaeologists have shown that a sophisticated Bronze Age culture began to develop as long as 5,000 years ago, reaching a glorious height between 300 BC and 200 AD.

No one knows why this culture declined and disappeared. What is known is that in the early centuries AD, people from India had begun to settle the region, bringing with them first the Hindu religion and then the Buddhist to augment the animistic worship of the earlier inhabitants.

(In fact, the three are freely blended. Thais follow the liberating philosophy of Therevada Buddhism, which is closest to the Buddha's original teaching and emphasizes good action and speech, nonviolence and loving kindness; but their monasteries, temples, homes and ceremonies include Hindu gods such as Vishnu, as well as various nature gods and household spirits.)

During those early centuries AD also, other ancestors of the Thai people arrived in the region, probably from southwestern China. They settled large expanses of land, forming shifting alliances with the various kingdoms— Mon, Lao and Khmer—of the area. In 1238, the Thais overthrew the dominant Khmer and proceeded to establish their own kingdom in the northwestern part of the central plain;

its capital was known as Sukhothai.

By 1351, the Thais had developed their greatest early state, known as Siam, and ruled from the city of Ayutthaya, north of Bangkok. Built on an island in the Chao Phraya River, Ayutthaya was a marvel, with many kilometres of canals, or klongs, crowded with waterborne markets, gilded temples and palaces and—according to the ambassadors of Louis XIV of France—jewel-encrusted statues of the Buddha cast in solid gold.

Both Sukhothai and Ayutthaya are splendid ruins now, but their spires and palaces, monasteries, temples and sculptures show the might of early Siam, which became the most powerful kingdom of Southeast Asia. Through centuries of Asian wars and European encroachments, astute leaders and a strong government that was centred on the sacred person of the King kept it independent.

In 1767, Burmese enemies destroyed Ayutthaya. But the Thais soon rallied under a new general, Taksin, ousted the invaders and began the present dynasty by founding a new capital further south at Thonburi, later moved to a nearby river settlement known as Bangkok, or "village of the wild plum trees". That is its name to foreigners today; the Thais call their capital Krungthep, meaning "City of Deities" or, more beautifully, "City of Angels". Thanks to intelligent rulers, the capital and kingdom have survived, reforming and adjusting to the modern era; in 1939, the country's name was changed to Thailand to reflect its proud history: the word means "land of the free".

Astuteness, flexibility and a strong national feeling have kept the country

free. As the buildings in its ancient cities—and the people of today—reveal, Thailand has absorbed the characteristics of many different cultures. In the south, near Malaysia, there are Islamic Thais; the hill tribes of the mountainous north still worship their own gods; the Chinese who crowd the cities follow their own forms of Buddhism. All of them together form a harmonious whole. The same can be said of their creative arts, including the art of cookery.

An old man celebrates the King's birthday, December 5, in Bangkok. Although the monarchy is now constitutional, Thais revere their ruler as a semi-divine being.

Gilded sculptures adorn Chiangmai's Wat Doi Suthep. This famous northern monastery houses a relic of the Buddha that is believed to have miraculous powers.

Vendors trim cabbages to sell in a Chiangmai market. Beautiful presentation is characteristic of Thai food stalls.

A Complex Cuisine

Thais do not divide meals into courses as Europeans do. Instead, everything is served at once, so that diners can pick and choose, making a Thai table a bright array of texture and colour. The centrepiece of a main meal is always a large bowl of steaming rice. Ranged round it are clear soups, spicy sauces and a variety of vegetable, meat, fish and seafood dishes.

The choice of dishes and the diners' choice about what to eat and in what order is guided by balance, a clear indication of the influence of the Chinese principles of Yin and Yang; the idea is to achieve an overall healthful harmony by balancing opposing qualities. So, for example, a mild-flavoured dish requires a spicy companion; a liquid dish something crisp and dry; grilled food may be accompanied by something steamed.

And ingredients and colours should be as diverse as possible.

Preparing such a table need not be difficult. Examples of dishes to choose are shown in the menus on pages 138 to 139, but you can make your own substitutions, and invent your own menus, keeping the principle of balance in mind. You may decide to cook as few as two dishes plus rice, or as many as 20, depending on whether you are serving a family dinner or presenting a large banquet, and on how much time and help you have.

Cooking the meal, whether it is large or small, requires only a basic understanding of Thai flavourings and some advance preparation. Certain vegetables, herbs, spices and other flavourings—available at large supermarkets or at Asian food stores—appear constantly in Thai recipes. Many of these are discussed in boxes or notes throughout this book, and include chilies (*page 31*) for heat; coconut milk (*page 135*) for sweet creaminess; coriander (*page 47*) for its distinctive scent; and lemon grass and kaffir lime leaves (*page 58*) for their sharpness. Curry pastes and hot sauces, such as the many versions of *nam prik*, can be made at home following the recipes on pages 26 to 37, but they are also available ready-made from Asian stores, as is the indispensible *nam plah* fish sauce.

Other common flavourings include garlic, ginger, pepper, rice vinegar and soy sauce. Thai vegetables are frequently stir-fried in a wok; this method of cooking ensures that they stay crisp and retain their colour, shape, flavour and goodness. Any vegetable oil can be used for frying except olive oil, whose taste does not complement the cuisine.

Preparation of the dishes should be organized in advance: most are very quickly made, allowing the cook more time to enjoy the meal. This is a light, extremely healthy cuisine that focuses on vegetables; these—and all other ingredients—should be as fresh as possible. Well in advance of cooking, they can be cut small (for quick, even frying or steaming); flavourings should be ready to hand. Thais love to ornament dishes with intricately cut fruits and vegetables (*page 97*); these, too, can be prepared in advance.

Utensils are those found in most kitchens: saucepans, frying pans, a pan for deep frying, chopping boards, meat mincers or grinders, strainers and different-sized kitchen knives. While you can use any large frying pan for stir-frying, a wok, with its generous proportions and smooth, sloping sides,

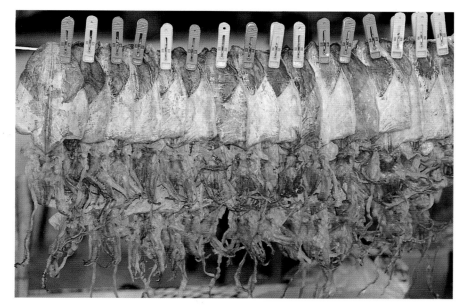

is better and makes the process easy.

Thai cooks depend on mortars and pestles for grinding ingredients; but a food processor or blender will speed up most jobs. You may want to dedicate a coffee grinder to the job of pulverizing spices. And you will need a saucepan with a tight-fitting lid—or an electric rice cooker—for rice.

For steaming vegetables or dishes such as glutinous rice balls (*page 51*), you need a bamboo or metal steamer. Alternatively, you can improvise by inverting a cup in a large pan filled with about 3 cm water and balancing a plate with the food on it on top .

Dried squid pegged to a line hang at a market stall. Customers can have them grilled on the spot, to eat for a snack.

Fish and shellfish sold in a Bangkok market. The Gulf of Thailand and Andaman Sea provide the country with an abundance of fresh seafood.

Similar in taste to lychees, the hairy-skinned rambutans are a popular tropical fruit.

A Special Joy in Food

As the following pages show, each of the four main regions of Thailand—the northwest, the northeast, the centre and the south—has its own specialities; however, they all share a distinctive approach to spices and other flavourings. The cookery uses very little fat and, because the majority of the people are Buddhist, there are many meatless dishes; in fact, because some forms of Buddhism forbid the slaughtering of animals, most Thai butchers are Muslims or Chinese.

Some Thai dishes, though originating in a particular region, are so well known that they are served throughout the kingdom. These include *Tom yam gung*, Fiery prawn soup (*page 56*), *Pat thai gung sot*, Stir-fried noodles (*page 87*) and *Yam neua*, Beef salad with coriander (*page 89*).

Thais share an easy-going approach to dining. During the heat of the day, eating is mostly a matter of consuming a succession of small, tasty snacks. Sold in large markets by vendors (whose stalls may consist only of one little chair and table), by food shops or by cooks who travel the streets and canals, such foods are available in a bewildering variety.

At lunchtime, it might be a curry with rice. Or a choice of grilled meats, various vegetable dishes and crisp salads, followed by a wonderful array of sweets. But city-dwellers also often prefer a late breakfast on their way to work, which they might buy from one of the countless street-corner noodle or soup stalls.

It is generally only in the evening, when the air has cooled, that families gather to eat together. Firm invitations to friends are rare, but those who drop by almost always stay on to enjoy a meal; that is the reason why Thai cooks usually prepare more rice than is strictly necessary. Leftovers can always be used up the next day.

Before dinner, everyone showers or

at least has a thorough handwashing, because cleanliness is a religious obligation. People sit where they like, often around a mat or carpet spread on the floor. Because pointing one's feet at someone is considered discourteous, men sit cross-legged; women kneel with their feet tucked under them.

The meal begins, and usually continues, with glasses of cold water. Some Thais drink chilled beer or Thai whiskey with their food, but few drink wine, which is expensive, and in any case would be overwhelmed by the spicy food. Every diner picks and chooses a few bites from one of the various dishes spread out before him, then moves on to the next dish, until everyone is satisfied. Only dessert is served separately.

Before the 19th century, when knives and forks appeared from Europe, Thais ate artfully with the fingers of

the right hand. They still sometimes do this, especially in rural areas and in the northern provinces, where glutinous rice, easy to form into little balls for dipping in sauce, is the main staple. Chinese chopsticks appear only for noodle dishes or for soups which contain noodles.

A colourful variety of enticing dishes awaits the hungry passer-by in a Bangkok market.

A woman walks along a lane in her northern village. Houses are traditionally built on stilts to protect the inhabitants from the monsoon damp.

The Northwest: A Mountain Life

Spread over the southern Himalayas bordering Burma, northwest Thailand, known as Lanna Thai, is a rugged, rather isolated area of thickly wooded mountain ranges. It was not linked to the rest of Thailand by rail until 1921, and its hill tribes speak their own dialect and still wear their distinctive dress and rich silver jewellery. Among these tribes, many of whom migrate back and forth across the Burmese border, are the Khmer, Lao and Mon, as well as more remote peoples such as the Lawa, who may have been Thailand's original inhabitants, driven into high country centuries ago.

This is the region of the Golden Triangle, where the opium poppy is still a major crop, cultivated by Meo tribespeople; the cooler climate, however, encourages the growth of other plants, including glutinous rice and more recently introduced foods such as tea, coffee, grapes, peaches, apples and strawberries, not to mention many vegetables.

It is an area rich in history, which is visible everywhere from the mountain caves with their remains of prehistoric peoples to the centuries-old wats, or temple and monastery complexes, of the principle city, Chiangmai. Lying in the shadow of Doi Inthanon, the region's highest peak, it is Thailand's second largest city but pretty and tranquil nevertheless. Capital of the northern kingdom of Lao from 1296, Chiangmai had years of independence or union with its powerful Burmese neighbour; Thailand was unable to absorb it until the 18th century, and its ancient architecture reflects centuries of Burmese influence, especially in the wats with their gilded spires and arches and wonderful sculptures. Traditional crafts, including items made from silk, carved teak and silver as well as such charming objects as painted paper parasols are still sold in Chiangmai's famous night-time market.

Venerable festivals, too, still abound; in fact those of northern Thailand are considered the finest in the kingdom. February, for instance, brings Chiangmai's flower festival, with parades of gloriously adorned floats. New Year, or Song Kran, is celebrated from April 13 to 15 with boisterous abandon. People drench each other with huge buckets of water, the idea being to encourage the rains.

Loy Drathong, the harvest festival that ends the rainy season with homage to an old goddess, the Mother of Rivers—celebrated throughout the country—is marked here by the release of brightly-coloured hot air balloons, that sail into the distant sky, taking all worries and troubles with them.

As for dining, northerners share the pleasure-loving approach of all the Thais, but in their own style, called *kantoke*. The word refers to the low red lacquer or woven bamboo tables diners place beside them on the floor to hold the dishes. A dinner will often include traditional regional dancing, with dancers in picturesque costumes. Among the charming choreographies are one for a sword dance and another for a candle dance.

These northern meals centre on glutinous rice rather than on the boiled rice of the lowlands. To go with it there are rather mild curries, many sauces and a range of traditional mountain dishes. Famous throughout the country are the hot, garlicky sausages of Chiangmai, whose citizens are the nation's premier pork cooks; these sausages are sold wrapped in banana leaves and tied with bamboo slivers. And the Thai-Burmese dish of crispy

fried noodles with a soup of coconut and curry is now made everywhere in Thailand.

More local is dog, the meat coming from a similar breed to the chow of China. Other specialities include fried cicadas, cows' placentas and giant water beetles that, crushed, give a highly individual flavour to some dishes.

The arrival of visitors at a remote area arouses a delighted curiosity in these village children.

A trainer gives an elephant and its calf a bath. Elephants are schooled for work from the age of three years.

Visitors cross over the wilderness on a traditional suspension bridge in the Khao Yai National Park, a nature reserve of 2,200 square kilometres.

The Northeast: A Khmer Legacy

Isan, Thailand's northeast corner, is enfolded on three sides by Laos and Cambodia. The region is a rolling plain, known as the Khorat Plateau, bordered by mountains. Life is hard here: the soil is sandy and poor, and droughts alternate with heavy monsoon rains, during which the Mekong River on the Laotian border rises in devastating floods. Most people are poor farmers raising jute, cattle and glutinous rice, and although government programmes are improving their situation, many of them migrate south to the cities in search of work as taxi drivers or as unskilled labour.

Life was not always so bleak. Less than a thousand years ago northeast Thailand was a rich and thickly wooded area; it was a major outpost of the splendid Khmer Empire of Cambodia, which ruled much of Southeast Asia from the ninth to the 15th centuries. The empire's capital was Cambodia's fabled city of Angkhor, now a jungle-covered ruin.

The legacy of those years is scattered throughout Isan in the form of great temple complexes. Clearly showing how the Khmer moved from Hindu to Buddhist belief, these complexes usually centre on the tiered towers known as *prangs*, which represent Mount Meru, home of the Hindu gods; often the *prangs* are surrounded by elaborate networks of canals and ponds to symbolize the world ocean. All of them, with their beautiful stonework and sculpture, were converted to Buddhist worship.

Among the most famous is Prasat Hin Phimai, near the town of Phimai; it is one of the finest surviving examples of classic Khmer architecture, dating from the early 12th century. But there are also many others to see.

The people of Isan, who still use many of these great temples, are farmers whose lives are bound by the natural rhythms of planting and harvest, and largely unaffected by the modern age. Despite the hardships of their way of life, northeasterners are friendly, with a great zest for life

Bicycle rickshaws, or samlors, are still traditional transport, as here in Nongkhai on the Mekong River.

and a strong tradition of music, folk dancing and festivals that offers welcome relief from the daily struggle for survival on the land.

A high point of the year is Bun Bong Fai, held during the second week of May in Yasothorn. Dedicated to the god of the clouds, this is a rainmakers' feast; at its climax, homemade rockets nearly nine metres long are launched into the sky accompanied by prayers for rain. A festival at full moon in July in Nongkhai, near the Laotian border, features boat races on the Mekong River.

And perhaps the most famous of all celebrations in Isan is the elephant round-up at Surin in November. In Thailand, there are still wild elephants as well as many trained ones, which are used as working animals in difficult terrain such as rainforests. At Surin, the beasts and their owners show their

skills in displays of dexterity at work and play. Especially famous is an elephant tug of war, for which the animal teams are lavishly painted and adorned. Another November event is the annual fair and silk market at Khonkaen, where visitors can buy lengths of brilliantly dyed Thai silk.

As for food, the people of this region, like their western neighbours, prefer glutinous rice. Meat is in short supply here, so many of the dishes are based on the abundant freshwater fish. Almost all Isan dishes are searingly hot; a number of delicious preparations have become restaurant fixtures throughout the country.

As in any poor and remote region where food is scarce, there are peculiar specialities; here they include snacks of fried grasshoppers or maggots, grilled lizards, anteaters' eggs and snail curry.

Buddhist (left) and Hindu statues share the Wat Kuk Sculpture Park near Nongkhai. The two religions intermingle comfortably in Thailand.

Bangkok:
The City of Angels

Traditional wooden dwellings on stilts, inhabited by Bangkok's poorer citizens, are built out into the Chao Phraya River (right, above). Spiky-skinned durians—evil to smell but delicious to taste—ornament a city market stall (right, below).

The centre of government, the seat of the royal family and Thailand's gateway to the rest of the world, the city of Bangkok is a study in contrasts. Sited since 1782 on the great central plain of Thailand along the banks of the Chao Phraya River, the city has at its heart a vast palace and temple complex—a city within a city—whose most famous and beautiful building is the Wat Phra Kaeo, or Temple of the Emerald Buddha.

The 14th-century figure of the Buddha, captured from a Laotian king in the 18th century, is not made of emerald but carved from a piece of solid green jade. It is the premier national treasure in a country of treasures, and is the central symbol of Thai Buddhism and nationhood. At the beginning of each of the three Thai seasons, the king changes its ceremonial robes, from gilt, to solid gold to gold sprinkled with diamonds.

Spreading out beyond the walls of this old city is modern Bangkok, a noisy metropolis of tower blocks, building sites, motorbikes, taxis and buses. It is laced with canals and, surprisingly, fringed with fields and orchards, and dotted with pleasant green parks. But the symbols of Thai worship are never far away: the city has more than 400 temples and almost every house has its small outdoor spirit shrine.

Perhaps because of its dense population, Bangkok is the place in Thailand where one most feels the public delight in the yearly round of religious and royal festivals. Songkran, the Thai New Year in April, is celebrated mostly on the outskirts of

the city, where the traditional water throwing (to encourage rain) is still allowed, along with boat races and elaborate processions.

In May comes the ancient sowing ceremony, which takes place in the old city, in the square in front of the royal palace. During this important ritual, the ground is furrowed with a sacred plough, then a Harvest Lord, representing the king, sows it with rice grains from baskets of silver and gold.

The month of November brings Loy Krathong, the festival of floating lights, more beautifully celebrated here than in any other place. To placate the water spirits and wash their own sins away, people launch thousands of *krathongs*—tiny, lotus-shaped baskets filled with candles, incense sticks, flowers and coins—upon the river, so

Classical dancers in traditional costume wait in the wings. Highly trained, they enact tales from the Thai national epic.

that the water is filled with myriad points of twinkling lights.

There are many more festivals than these, of course, and many more gods: Bangkok is a tapestry made of all the strands of Thai culture. As well as the central Thai themselves, it has Muslim and Sikh communities and also many immigrants from the northeast, known as Thai Lao or Thai Isan. And there is an enormous and influential Chinese population, centred in the district of Sampeng, southeast of the old city, but spread throughout Bangkok.

All these people fit into the pleasant lifestyle of this tropical capital, emphasizing *sanuk*, or fun. And all add to the city's culinary delights: Bangkok is filled with bright, busy markets selling wonderful fruit, vegetables, meat and fish brought in from the surrounding countryside, as well as a

bewildering array of cooked food.

On the klongs that thread through western Bangkok, the food comes to the people in boats, which serve not only as markets but as floating snack bars. Vendors on boats sell fresh fruit or cooked sweet dishes—or they will fry an egg for a customer or mix him a curry. The same applies in the city's landbased markets, whose stalls sell everything from the fiery *lahp* (minced beef) or the dried lizard of northern Thailand to south Indian-style curries and Malaysian Muslim dishes.

And then there are the restaurants. These range from simple cookshops to elaborate, Chinese-style eating houses. There is even a restaurant so enormous that the waiters must wear roller skates. Everything good to eat is to be found in the city; Bangkok is truly a food lover's paradise.

Carved monkey warriors guard the tiled and gilded spires of Wat Phra Kaeo (top). This royal temple complex is among Thailand's holiest. Water taxis (above) navigate a klong, one of the canals of Bangkok.

Eroded by the waves, limestone monoliths rise from the sea off Thailand's western shore. This strange and beautiful region is a popular site for tourist excursions.

The South and Gulf of Thailand: Treasures of the Tropics

A long, narrow strip reaching towards Malaysia, its west coast facing the Andaman Sea and its east coast the Gulf of Thailand, southern Thailand is distinctly different from the rest of the nation. It is abundantly tropical, a region of mountain and orchid-filled rainforest, of palm-fringed beaches, jewel-like islands and clear, warm seas. It has a large Muslim population, especially in the areas bordering on Malaysia. In the towns, the domes and minarets of the mosques coexist comfortably with the curving gables of Buddhist temples.

The long, sandy beaches round the Gulf of Thailand make this coastline an important resort area. On the eastern side of the peninsula, Hua Hin has been famed for many decades. With its old-fashioned summer houses, turn-of-the-

century hotels and beautiful topiary gardens, it still remains a favourite. A major resort on the opposite coast of the Gulf provides a study in contrasts: Pattaya, a gaudy mixture of high-rise hotels, noisy discos and restaurants, has some claim to the title of Thailand's Miami Beach.

Farther south, the island of Phuket, off the western coast of the Thai peninsula, and the spectacular limestone pinnacles on the nearby mainland, are fast becoming major tourist attractions. Less developed, more peaceful islands include Ko Samui and Ko Samet. Not far from the latter—easy to find because of the smell of drying fish—is mainland Rayong, a home of Thai fish sauce.

Tourism is by no means the region's only source of income. The rubber tree, introduced from the Americas in the 19th century, flourishes here. It is to be found on vast plantations that make

Thailand the world's third largest producer of rubber. There are cashew and pineapple plantations, too, and large tracts of land that are given over to coconut growing. (Small, dexterous monkeys have been trained to help harvest this crop; seen at work, they are a remarkable sight.)

And of course, all along the coasts, fishermen in brightly painted boats ply the warm waters, producing a catch that helps feed the whole of Thailand: the men bring in lobsters and crayfish, prawns and mussels, as well as numerous delicious fish in a variety of shapes and sizes.

The people of the south are more Malaysian in feature than their northern counterparts, and they speak more quickly, with their own distinctive intonations. Like their countrymen, however, they know how to enjoy themselves at public festivals and rituals. In April, for instance, there is a shadow play competition in Phatthalung. This ancient art—there are references to it as early as 400 BC—seems to have reached Thailand from India; in it, the shadows of special puppet figures are thrown on a screen to enact classical dramas from the *Ramakien*, the national epic of Thailand.

In September, at Nakhon Si Thammarat, far south on the eastern side of the peninsula, there is a Buddhist festival of rituals honouring dead ancestors. And at Phuket, on the west coast, the region's large Chinese population provides a vegetarian festival in October, during which the faithful abstain from eating meat and demonstrate the powers of their faith to protect them by public ordeals

such as walking on burning coals.

As in the rest of Thailand, vegetables play an important part in the cuisine of the south, although perhaps not quite so centrally as the superb local seafood. This is available in abundance in the markets and in the restaurants, which specialize in delicious baskets of mixed seafood.

As might be expected, coconuts play a sizable role in southern cuisine, especially in soups—for example in *Tom kah gai*, Chicken soup with lemon grass (*page 52*) or in meat dishes such as *Gaeng massaman*, Beef curry (*page 64*); and coconut milk is used in many desserts. Another appealing southern speciality is cashew nuts, fried until golden and served as a snack.

A hammock provides an airy resting place on the island of Phi Phi Don.

Rubber from the great plantations of the southeast awaits export at Sonkghla.

CURRY PASTES, SAUCES AND DIPS

Various herbs, spices and other flavourings, crushed with a pestle and mortar (or ground together in a food processor) are the foundation of Thai cuisine. They are used in so many ways that it is a good idea to have them to hand, whether you buy them in a shop specializing in Asian foods or make them yourself following recipes in this chapter.

Chief among these mixtures are curry pastes, formed from different combinations of flavourings. A well-made paste is the basic ingredient of Thai curries and, in Thailand, recipes ranging from mild to extremely hot are handed down from one generation to the next. You may wish to make such pastes in large quantities and store them in the refrigerator, where they will keep for months. To save time and trouble, however, you can buy perfectly acceptable versions in Asian groceries.

Just as essential as the curry pastes is *nam plah*, a sauce made from fermented fish or seafood and used in place of salt. Enhanced with chili peppers, garlic, coriander and lime juice (*recipe, page 30*) the sauce acquires a wonderful flavour.

Besides acting as flavouring agents in cooked dishes, pastes and sauces are the basis for dips. These lend extra flavour to many foods, especially vegetables, raw or cooked.

Red curry paste

Basic recipe • Hot **Kreuang gaeng pet daeng** *Makes 1 bowl (serves 4)*

8 fresh red jalapeño chili peppers
3 fresh red bird's-eye chili peppers
3 shallots • 1 stalk fresh lemon grass
2 cm piece fresh galangal
2 coriander roots • 1 kaffir lime
1 tsp coriander seeds
½ tsp cumin seeds • 1 tsp salt
½ tsp freshly ground black pepper
½ tsp freshly grated nutmeg
1 tsp shrimp paste

Preparation time: 25 minutes
150 kJ/36 calories per portion

1 Wash all the chili peppers, discard the stalks and chop finely (*see Warning, below*). Peel and finely chop the shallots. Wash the lemon grass and cut into thin rings. Wash the galangal and coriander roots and chop finely. Wash the kaffir lime in hot water. Peel with a knife, then finely chop enough rind to fill a teaspoon.

2 Place the coriander seeds in a small frying pan without fat, and dry fry over high heat for about 2 minutes. Crush the cumin in a large mortar. Gradually add the rest of the ingredients and grind them together thoroughly. Add the salt, pepper and nutmeg and continue to grind to a creamy paste. Finally, stir in the shrimp paste.

Note: Red or green curry paste is a basic ingredient of most Thai curries. Instead of the jalapeños you could use small pimientos (*see Glossary*).

Green curry paste

Basic recipe • Very hot **Kreuang gaeng kiaw wahn** *Makes 1 bowl (serves 4)*

8 fresh green jalapeño chili peppers
3 fresh green bird's-eye chili peppers
3 shallots • 1 stalk fresh lemon grass
2 cm piece fresh galangal
2 coriander roots • 1 kaffir lime
1 tsp coriander seeds
½ tsp cumin seeds • 1 tsp salt
½ tsp freshly ground black pepper
½ tsp freshly grated nutmeg
1 tsp shrimp paste

1 This paste is prepared in the same way as red curry paste, using green chili peppers instead of the red ones.

Note: The traditional large pestle and mortar is the best way to make Thai curry pastes. Alternatively, you can grind the ingredients in a food processor—or an electric coffee grinder, kept specially for the purpose because of the overpowering flavours.

Warning: All chili peppers should be handled with care because they contain volatile oils that can irritate the skin and cause eyes to burn; so always wash your hands immediately after use.

Panaeng curry paste

Basic recipe • Hot **Kreuang gaeng panaeng** *Makes 1 bowl (serves 4)*

6 large dried chili peppers
1 tsp salt • 3 shallots • 3 garlic cloves
1 stalk fresh lemon grass
2 cm piece fresh galangal
2 coriander roots • 1 kaffir lime
½ tsp freshly ground black pepper
½ tsp shrimp paste

Preparation time: 20 minutes
140 kJ/33 calories per portion

1 Cut the chilies in half crosswise, discard the stalks and soak in lukewarm water for about 5 minutes. Drain and squeeze out excess moisture. Crush the chilies and the salt with a mortar and pestle (*see Warning, above*).

2 Peel and finely chop the shallots and garlic. Wash the lemon grass and cut into thin rings. Wash and finely chop the galangal and coriander roots. Wash the kaffir lime in hot water. Peel with a knife, then finely chop enough of the rind to fill a teaspoon.

3 Add the chopped ingredients to the chilies in the mortar and crush everything thoroughly. Finally, mix in the ground black pepper and shrimp paste and stir to a fine paste.

Massaman curry paste

Kreuang gaeng massaman

Basic recipe • Southern Thailand

Makes 1 bowl (serves 4)

8 large dried red chili peppers (see Glossary)
2 cm piece fresh galangal
1 stalk fresh lemon grass
5 shallots
10 garlic cloves
1 tbsp coriander seeds
1 tsp cumin seeds
½ tsp ground cloves
1 tsp ground cinnamon
1 tsp ground star anise
½ tsp freshly ground black pepper
1 tsp shrimp paste

Preparation time: 25 minutes

230 kJ/55 calories per portion

1 Halve the chili peppers lengthwise. Discard the stalks and seeds, then soak them in lukewarm water for about 5 minutes. Drain and squeeze them to remove excess moisture. Wash the galangal and lemon grass. Thinly slice the galangal, and cut the lemon grass into thin rings. Peel and finely chop the shallots and garlic.

2 Dry fry the coriander and cumin seeds in a frying pan over medium heat for about 3 minutes, until they give off a spicy aroma; remove and set aside. Dry fry the galangal, lemon grass, shallots and garlic in the pan over medium heat for about 5 minutes, stirring occasionally, until browned.

3 Grind the coriander and cumin seeds with a pestle in a mortar, then gradually add the chilies and fried ingredients and pound them to a paste. Add the ground cloves, cinnamon, star anise, black pepper and shrimp paste and mix thoroughly.

Note: The Indian influence on Thai cuisine is reflected in this curry paste, which often also include cardamom seeds. It is used mainly with beef and chicken but, because it is a great favourite with Thailand's Muslim community, not with pork.

Yellow curry paste

Kreuang gaeng garee

Basic recipe • Hot

Makes 1 bowl (serves 4)

5 large dried red chili peppers (see Glossary)
2 cm piece fresh galangal
1 stalk fresh lemon grass
5 shallots
10 garlic cloves
1 tsp salt
1 tbsp coriander seeds
1 tsp cumin seeds
1 tbsp curry powder
1 tsp shrimp paste

Preparation time: 25 minutes

230 kJ/55 calories per portion

1 Cut the chili peppers in half crosswise, discard the stalks and soak in lukewarm water for about 5 minutes. Drain and squeeze them to remove excess moisture.

2 Wash the galangal and lemon grass. Thinly slice the galangal, and cut the lemon grass into thin rings. Peel and finely chop the shallots and garlic.

3 Place the galangal, lemon grass, shallots and garlic in a frying pan and dry fry, stirring continuously, for about 3 minutes. Leave to cool a little.

4 Crush the halved chili peppers and the salt with a pestle in a large mortar. Gradually add the fried ingredients and pound vigorously into a paste. Stir in the curry powder and shrimp paste.

Note: Cumin, which has a pungent and rather bitter flavour, is a popular spice throughout Southeast Asia and India. It is available in whole seed or powdered form from good supermarkets and Asian food stores.

Chili sauce with coriander

Nam plah prik

*4 fresh red bird's-eye chili peppers
(see Glossary)
2 garlic cloves
3 tbsp fish sauce (nam plah)
2 tbsp lime juice (or, if unavailable,
lemon juice)
1 stalk fresh coriander*

Preparation time: 15 minutes

56 kJ/13 calories per portion

1 Wash the chili peppers, discard the stalks and cut into thin rings or crush with a pestle and mortar. Transfer to a small bowl. Peel and finely chop the garlic. Add the garlic, the fish sauce and the lime juice to the chilies, and stir them all together.

2 Wash the coriander and shake dry. Finely chop the stalk and leaves and add to the chili sauce.

Variation: You can also add very thin slices of shallot or red onion to the sauce.

Note: Chili sauce is very popular throughout Thailand. It goes well with any fried rice dish and is also suitable for fried vegetables and meat dishes where there is little sauce as, for example, Pork fillet with pineapple (*page 74*) or Roast duck (*page 111*). It is important that the sauce is freshly made and not kept for long.

Chili peppers

Chili peppers, together with other members of the *Capsicum* family such as sweet red and green peppers, were native to Central and South America as early as 9,000 years ago. They were brought to Europe by Columbus at the end of the 15th century and taken, soon after, to Southeast Asia and the East Indies by the Portuguese.

Chilies come in all sorts of shapes, sizes and colours. The smaller they are the hotter they tend to be and some of the hottest chilies grow In Thailand. The tiny red bird's-eye chili, *prik kee noo*, is the most fiery of all. The larger red or green *prik kee fah* is milder, as are pickled chilies. Dried chili peppers are hotter than fresh ones.

Chili peppers contain carbohydrates and protein, calcium, iron and vitamins A and C. The hot taste stems from a substance called capsaicin, which can irritate the skin and cause eyes to burn, and in some people produces strong allergic reactions. It is important to remember to wash your hands immediately after handling chilies.

To bring out their flavour, chilies should be finely chopped or crushed with a pestle and mortar. Thais like to use the whole chili, including the seeds, but to reduce the "heat" you can remove the seeds before use.

Sweet-sour-hot sauce

Basic recipe • Aromatic

Nam jim priaw wahn

Makes 1 bowl (serves 4)

½ **sweet red pepper**
1 **garlic clove**
2 **fresh red bird's-eye chili peppers**
(see Glossary)
10 **tbsp rice vinegar (or, if**
unavailable, mild wine vinegar)
10 **tbsp sugar**

Preparation time: 15 minutes
(plus 30 minutes' cooking time)

660 kJ/160 calories per portion

1 Derib and deseed the sweet pepper half, then wash and pat dry. Peel the garlic. Discard the stalk from the chili peppers, then wash and pat dry.

2 Crush the sweet pepper, garlic and chili peppers with a pestle and mortar, then transfer the crushed ingredients to a small saucepan.

3 Add about ¼ litre water, the rice vinegar and the sugar, then bring to the boil. Reduce the heat to medium and cook, uncovered, for about 30 minutes, until the sauce thickens slightly.

Variation: Cucumber can be added to this sauce. Peel a piece of cucumber, cut it lengthwise into quarters, then slice it very thinly and add to the other ingredients. You could also stir in some chopped peanuts.

Simple chili sauce

Quick and easy • Very hot

Nam jim prik bon

Makes 1 bowl (serves 4)

2 **garlic cloves**
4 **tbsp fish sauce (nam plah)**
2 **tbsp lime juice**
1 **tbsp palm sugar, or soft**
brown sugar
1 **tbsp chili powder**

Preparation time: 10 minutes

89 kJ/21 calories per portion

1 Peel the garlic and crush with a pestle and mortar.

2 Add the fish sauce, lime juice, palm sugar and chili powder. Stir until the sugar dissolves.

Variations: Instead of lime juice, you can use tamarind juice. Soak a walnut-sized piece of tamarind in 5 tbsp warm water for about 10 minutes, then knead the pulp thoroughly and squeeze out the juice. Or, instead of fresh garlic, you can use finely sliced pickled garlic (*page 35*), doubling the quantity.

Note: This version of chili sauce is mainly eaten in northeastern Thailand, where it is used as a dip for homemade balls of glutinous rice.

Chilies in vinegar

Very quick • Refreshing

Prik nam som

Makes 1 bowl (serves 4)

1 **fresh red jalapeño chili pepper**
1 **fresh green jalapeño chili pepper**
12.5 **cl white rice vinegar (or, if not**
available, mild wine vinegar)

Preparation time: 5 minutes
40 kJ/9 calories per portion

1 Wash and dry the chili peppers and discard the stalks. Cut them into rings and put them in a bowl. Add the vinegar and stir.

Note: In Thailand, *Prik nam som* is often made with hot chili peppers. The jalapeños give it a somewhat milder taste; to make it even milder, you could use small pimientos (Spanish peppers). The sauce can be served with any noodle dish, and also as a condiment to season other food at the table.

Pickled garlic

Gratiam dong

Simple · Spicy

Serves 20

60 cl white rice vinegar (or, if unavailable, mild wine vinegar)
600 g sugar
1 tsp salt
500 g small garlic heads

Preparation time: 30 minutes (plus 1 week's marinating time)

680 kJ/162 calories per portion

1 Bring the vinegar, sugar, salt and 60 cl water to the boil in a saucepan, reduce the heat to low and simmer for about 10 minutes. Leave to cool.

2 Remove the outer skin from the garlic heads, leaving the cloves intact. Wash and drain them thoroughly.

3 Rinse out a large preserving jar with boiling water and leave to drain. Place the garlic heads in the jar and top up with the cooled vinegar and sugar solution. Close the jar and leave to stand in a cool place for about 1 week.

Note: Pickled garlic should be peeled before using as an ingredient or condiment. It will keep in the jar for more than a year and can be served with many Thai dishes.

Shrimp paste dip

Nam prik gapi

Simple · Hot

Serves 4

2 tbsp dried shrimps · 4 garlic cloves
4 fresh bird's-eye chili peppers (see Glossary)
2 tbsp shrimp paste · 4 tbsp lime juice
1 tbsp fish sauce (nam plah)
3 tbsp palm, or other brown, sugar

Preparation time: 20 minutes

330 kJ/79 calories per portion

1 Finely crush the dried shrimps with a pestle and mortar. Place in a small bowl and reserve. Peel the garlic. Wash the chili peppers and discard the stalks. Crush the garlic, chili peppers and shrimp paste in a mortar.

2 Transfer the mixture to a bowl. Add the lime juice, crushed shrimps, fish sauce and sugar, and stir to a smooth paste. Season with more lime juice and sugar if necessary.

Note: This dip is good with all raw, fried and boiled or steamed vegetables.

Peanut sauce

Nam jim moo satay

Simple · Aromatic

Makes 1 bowl (serves 4)

150 g salted, roasted peanuts
3 tbsp oil
2 tbsp red curry paste (page 26)
1 can (40 cl) unsweetened coconut milk
3 tbsp brown sugar · 1 tsp salt
3 tbsp rice vinegar

Preparation time: 25 minutes
1500 kJ/360 calories per portion

1 Finely crush the peanuts with a pestle and mortar. Heat the oil in a small saucepan over medium heat and cook the red curry paste until lightly browned.

2 Stir in the coconut milk and cook for about 1 minute. Add the peanuts, sugar, salt and vinegar, reduce the heat to low and simmer for about 15 minutes, until creamy.

Note: This sauce is served with Pork satay (*page 73*). If making fresh curry paste, allow an extra 25 minutes' preparation time.

Tomato and minced meat dip

Nam prik ong

Not difficult • Northern Thailand

Serves 4

5 large dried chili peppers (see Glossary)
3 medium-sized tomatoes
1 stalk fresh lemon grass
3 stalks fresh coriander
5 shallots
10 garlic cloves
2 tsp salt
1 tsp shrimp paste
75 g lean minced pork
75 g lean minced beef
3 tbsp oil
1 tsp sugar
1 tbsp lime juice

Preparation time: 25 minutes

940 kJ/220 calories per portion

1 Remove the stalks from the chili peppers and cut them in half crosswise. Soak them in lukewarm water for about 5 minutes, then drain and squeeze out excess moisture.

2 Wash and dry the tomatoes, then slice or coarsely dice them. Wash the lemon grass and cut into thin rings. Wash, shake dry and finely chop the coriander. Peel the shallots and garlic. Cut the shallots into quarters.

3 Crush the chili peppers and the salt with a pestle in a mortar. Add 5 of the garlic cloves to the mortar and crush them, then gradually add the shallots, lemon grass, coriander and shrimp paste and pound them into a paste. Add the minced meat and stir vigorously.

4 Finely chop the remaining garlic cloves. Heat the oil in a frying pan over medium heat and fry the chopped garlic for about 2 minutes until golden. Add the pounded meat paste, the tomatoes, sugar and lime juice and stir-fry over medium heat for about 5 minutes, until all the liquid has evaporated.

Note: This dip is served with raw or cooked vegetables. If you like, you can plunge the tomatoes briefly in boiling water and skin them. In Thailand, however, they are never skinned.

Hot prawn dip

Nam prik num

Fairly easy • Northern Thailand

Serves 4

2 fresh red jalapeño chili peppers,
or small pimientos (see Glossary)
1 fresh green jalapeño chili pepper,
or small pimiento (see Glossary)
10 garlic cloves
5 shallots
1 tbsp oil
300 g medium-sized whole
raw prawns
3 tbsp fish sauce (nam plah)
3 tbsp lime juice

Preparation time: 40 minutes

*560 kJ/130 calories
per portion*

1 Wash the chili peppers, remove the stalks and chop coarsely. Peel and finely chop the garlic and shallots. Heat the oil in a frying pan over medium heat and fry the chilies, garlic and shallots for about 5 minutes, until dark brown.

2 Rinse the prawns in cold water. Bring ¼ litre water to the boil in a saucepan. Add the prawns and boil for about 2 minutes. Drain, reserving a little of the stock, and leave the prawns to cool. Set 2 prawns aside for garnish and shell the rest, removing the heads and tails and the dark vein-like intestines. Chop the flesh very finely.

3 Coarsely crush the chilies and shallot mixture with a pestle in a mortar. Add the chopped prawns and stir briefly. Transfer to a small bowl, and stir in the fish sauce, lime juice and the reserved prawn stock. The dip should have a thick consistency. Garnish with the reserved prawns.

Note: This dip is delicious with raw or cooked vegetables.

SNACKS AND SOUPS

Snacking is a way of life in Thailand. A constant supply of spicy titbits is always available from food markets or street traders, sheltering from the blazing sun—or monsoon rains—under large colourful umbrellas, or from travelling vendors who have converted their motorbikes into movable kitchens. Noodle boats, or *guay tiaw reua*, ply the canals; pedlars carrying entire meals in baskets slung on poles across their shoulders wander the streets.

Many of these tempting dishes can be made at home, as the following pages show. They include various small savoury pastries, such as the Thai version of spring rolls (*page 40*), meatballs and rice balls, seafood and delicious salads. Thai soups, quickly prepared, are usually based on light broths, many of which include coconut milk, lending them a creamy sweet taste. Other soup ingredients range from noodles to meat, and spicing can vary from mild to fiery.

You can serve any of these dishes as a snack or as part of a main meal. If you wish to serve separate courses, these make excellent starters. Alternatively, a selection of snacks served together can form a light summer meal.

Spring rolls
Bo-bia

Fairly easy • Most occasions

Serves 4 to 6

100 g cellophane noodles
100 g white cabbage
1 small carrot (about 50 g)
2 garlic cloves
1 litre vegetable oil
125 g minced pork
125 g minced beef
2 tbsp fish sauce (nam plah)
1 tsp sugar
2 tbsp oyster sauce
20 frozen spring roll wrappers,
about 20 cm square, thawed
1 egg white, lightly beaten
1 bowl sweet-sour-hot sauce
(page 32)

For garnish (optional):
lettuce leaves, slices cucumber and
tomato

Preparation time: 1 hour
(plus 45 minutes for the sauce)

2,200 kJ/450 calories per portion
(if serving 6)

1 Soak the cellophane noodles in warm water for about 10 minutes. Cut them into short strips with kitchen scissors (*above*), then drain and set aside.

2 Wash and trim the white cabbage, removing the core, and shred it finely. Peel and shred the carrot. Peel the garlic cloves.

3 Heat 2 tbsp of the oil in a frying pan or wok. Crush the garlic into the pan and fry briefly until lightly browned. Add the minced meat and stir-fry over low heat for about 2 minutes, until cooked through. Add the shredded cabbage and carrot and the noodles (*above*). Season with the fish sauce, sugar and oyster sauce, and continue frying for a further 3 minutes. Remove from the heat and leave to cool.

4 Lay the dough wrappers on a work surface and place 2 tbsp of the filling in the centre of each. Fold one end corner of the wrapper over the filling (*above*).

5 Fold one side over, then the other side—the roll should be about 7 cm long—then roll up tightly (*above*). Brush the inside edge of the end of the wrapper with a little egg white and rub down firmly to seal the roll.

6 Heat the remaining vegetable oil in a wok or deep frying pan until sizzling. Fry the spring rolls in batches for about 3 minutes until golden-brown, then remove. Drain on kitchen paper and keep them warm. Serve hot, garnished, if you like, with lettuce leaves and slices of cucumber and tomato, and accompanied by the sweet-sour-hot sauce.

Meatballs with pineapple

Ma hor

More complex • Special occasions

Serves 4 to 6

200 g medium-sized raw prawns
100 g salted, roasted peanuts
2 tbsp vegetable oil
100 g minced pork
100 g minced beef
5 garlic cloves
3 sprigs fresh coriander
½ tsp freshly ground black pepper
350 g palm sugar (or, if unavailable,
soft brown sugar)
1 tsp salt
1 medium-sized pineapple

Preparation time: 1½ hours

2,300 kJ/550 calories per portion
(if serving 6)

1 Shell the prawns, removing the heads and dark, vein-like intestines. Wash, pat dry and chop finely. Crush the peanuts in a mortar or food processor and set aside.

2 Heat the oil in a frying pan and cook the chopped prawns and minced pork and beef over medium heat for 15 to 20 minutes, until the pan juices have evaporated. Remove prawns and meat from the pan and set aside.

3 Peel the garlic. Wash the coriander and shake dry. Separate the stalks and leaves; reserve the leaves. Pound the garlic, coriander stalks and pepper together in a mortar to make a paste.

4 In a small saucepan, slowly heat the sugar until it is a thick liquid. Add the garlic paste and stir thoroughly. Stir in the peanuts, minced meat, prawns and salt and simmer for 25 to 30 minutes until the mixture becomes firm. Remove from the heat and allow to cool.

5 Peel the pineapple and remove the brown eyes. Cut it into eight slices, remove the core, then cut the slices into bite-sized chunks. Arrange the pineapple pieces on a large serving dish and top each with a little ball of the meat-and-prawn mixture. Garnish with the coriander leaves and serve.

Variation: Instead of pineapple, use segments of orange, first removing the rind and pith.

Pineapples

Native to Central and South America but long established in Asia—Thailand is a leading exporter—pineapples are one of the most decorative table fruits. When they were first introduced to Europe during the 16th century, their exotic shape caused a sensation, even inspiring architectural ornament. The fragrant yellow flesh is a popular ingredient in Thai cooking, where it is used in both sweet and savoury dishes.

Pineapples are available all year round and best when eaten fresh. They have a high sugar content—about 15 per cent—but are also rich in minerals and vitamins.

When buying a pineapple, look for a sweet-smelling fruit with an even brownish-yellow skin and no green patches. To test if it is ripe, tap the base: a dull, solid sound indicates ripeness and the flesh should also give slightly when pressed. A ripe pineapple will keep for two to three days in the refrigerator.

If fresh pineapple is unavailable, the unsweetened canned fruit is a good and easy-to-use substitute.

Meat and prawn parcels

Bo-bia saweuy

Serves 4

50 g white radish (mooli)
1 bowl sweet-sour-hot sauce
(page 32)
500 g medium-sized raw prawns
75 g minced pork
75 g minced beef
3 tbsp light soy sauce
½ tsp freshly ground black pepper
1 tbsp cornflour
50 g unsalted cashew nuts
2 sprigs fresh coriander
8 rice-paper wrappers, about
20 cm square
4 tbsp light sesame seeds
1 egg white, lightly beaten
50 cl vegetable oil

For garnish (optional):
fresh pineapple, lettuce leaves

Preparation time: 45 minutes
(plus 45 minutes for the sauce)

2,700 kJ/640 calories per portion

1 Peel the radish and cut it into thin slices. Cut the slices into fine strips (*above*) and mix them into the sweet-sour-hot sauce.

2 Shell the prawns, removing the heads and dark vein-like intestines (*above*). Finely chop the prawns and mix thoroughly with the minced pork and beef, soy sauce, pepper and cornflour. Coarsely chop the cashew nuts. Wash the coriander, shake dry, and chop coarsely.

3 Immerse a rice-paper wrapper in hot water for about 30 seconds, until soft. Lay it on a worktop and spread it with a quarter of the meat and prawn paste, leaving a border of 1 to 2 cm.

4 Sprinkle the paste with a quarter of the cashew nuts, sesame seeds and chopped coriander (*above*). Brush the border with a little egg white, then wet and soften a second wrapper and lay it on top. Press the two wrappers firmly together round the edge. Repeat the process to make three more parcels.

5 Heat the oil in a large frying pan over medium heat. Using a spatula, gently place the filled parcels, one at a time, in the oil, and fry for about 1 minute, turning once, until golden-brown. Remove and drain on kitchen paper. Cut each parcel into 8 pieces and place on a bed of lettuce leaves. Garnish, if you like, with pieces of fresh pineapple and serve with the radish in sweet-sour-hot sauce.

Note: Because rice paper is brittle and breaks easily, it should be soaked to soften it before use. You could, if you prefer, use spring roll wrappers (*page 40*) which do not need soaking.

Chili prawns

Not difficult · Hot   **Gung sah**   *Serves 4*

600 g medium-sized raw prawns
3 tbsp light soy sauce
½ tsp freshly ground black pepper
6 garlic cloves
5 sprigs fresh coriander
5 fresh bird's-eye chili peppers (see Glossary)
4 tbsp lime juice
3 tbsp sugar
4 tbsp fish sauce (nam plah)
3 tbsp vegetable oil

For garnish:
washed lettuce leaves

Preparation time: 30 minutes
(plus 20 minutes' marinating time)

960 kJ/230 calories per portion

1 Shell the prawns, removing the heads and dark, vein-like intestines but leaving the tails on. Wash and pat them dry, then mix with the soy sauce and pepper. Cover and leave to marinate in the refrigerator for about 20 minutes.

2 Meanwhile, peel the garlic. Wash the coriander and shake dry. Separate the leaves and the stalks and reserve both. Wash the chilies and remove the stalks.

3 Put the chilies, garlic and coriander stalks into a mortar and with a pestle pound them into a paste—or grind them with a food processor. Transfer the paste to a small bowl, and stir in the lime juice, sugar and fish sauce. Continue stirring until the sugar has completely dissolved.

4 Heat the oil in a frying pan over medium heat. Fry the prawns for about 3 minutes, until they turn red. Transfer them to a serving dish, pour over the sauce, and garnish with the lettuce and coriander leaves.

Note: You can also serve the chili sauce separately so that guests can help themselves. If you prefer your sauce less hot, halve the chilies before pounding and remove the seeds—or use milder chilies.

Coriander

Coriander, one of the most ancient herbs, is known to have been in use both as a flavouring and a medicinal plant as far back as 5000 BC; it first appeared in China around 200 BC.

Also known as Chinese parsley, the herb has a strong aromatic taste that is one of the staple flavourings of Far Eastern cuisine, particularly in Thailand. The feathery leaves are a favourite garnish and, together with the stalks, are used liberally to flavour soups, salads and meat or seafood dishes. The root is pounded and used in marinades and the seeds, which are very different in taste, are used as a spice to flavour curries.

Fresh coriander is widely available and can be found both in Asian food shops and in most good supermarkets and greengrocers. Or you can cultivate the herb yourself from seed.

If stored in the refrigerator, with the roots in water and the leaves covered with a plastic bag, coriander will keep for several days. Chopped fresh coriander can also be frozen.

Chicken breast with lettuce

Not difficult • Special occasions **Miang gai** *Serves 4 to 6*

400 g boned chicken breast
3 tbsp fish sauce (nam plah)
2 tbsp lime juice
2 tbsp sugar
two 5 cm pieces fresh young ginger
10 shallots
5 fresh bird's-eye chili peppers
(see Glossary)
2 small green limes
50 g salted, roasted peanuts
1 iceberg lettuce

Preparation time: 45 minutes

610 kJ/150 calories per portion
(if serving 6)

1 Finely chop the chicken using a knife or a food processor. Place in a bowl together with the fish sauce (*above*), lime juice and sugar, and mix well. Cover the bowl and leave to marinate in the refrigerator for about 20 minutes.

2 Meanwhile, peel the ginger and the shallots, and cut into small dice. Wash the chilies, remove the stalks, then slice into thin rings. Wash the limes thoroughly in hot water or, if you prefer, peel them with a sharp knife, removing both the rind and the pith. Cut the fruit into small dice. Arrange the ginger, shallots, chilies, limes and peanuts in individual small bowls (*above*), or in separate piles on a large serving dish.

3 Tear the iceberg lettuce into pieces about 6 cm square. Wash and shake them dry and arrange the pieces on a large serving dish.

4 Wrap the chopped chicken in a dry, clean cloth and squeeze out the marinade into a saucepan. Bring the marinade briefly to the boil, stir in the chicken and cook over medium heat for about 2 minutes. Remove the pan from the heat and leave to cool.

5 With your hands, shape the chicken into walnut-sized pieces (*above*), squeezing out any remaining excess moisture, and place each one on a piece of lettuce. Serve, together with the bowls of chopped accompaniments.

Variations: Instead of chicken breast, use chopped fillets of fish such as coley, cod or redfish. You can also vary the type of lettuce, or use spinach leaves—or a combination of the two.

Fried prawns

Gung rampan

Not difficult • Crisp and delicious

Serves 4

500 g medium-sized raw prawns
3 tbsp light soy sauce
½ tsp freshly ground black pepper
100 g tempura flour
1 tsp salt
1 litre vegetable oil
1 bowl sweet-sour-hot sauce
(page 32)

Preparation time: 30 minutes
(plus 30 minutes' marinating time
and 45 minutes for the sauce)

2,000 kj/480 calories per portion

1 Shell the prawns, removing the heads and dark, vein-like intestines but leaving the tails on. Wash and pat them dry, then rub with the soy sauce and pepper. Cover and leave to marinate in the refrigerator for about 30 minutes.

2 Using an egg whisk, slowly whisk together the tempura flour, salt and about ¼ litre water until it becomes a thick, smooth batter.

3 Heat the oil in a large frying pan or wok; it is hot enough when small bubbles rise from a wooden spoon-handle dipped into the oil.

4 Hold the prawns by the tail and pull them through the batter so that they are coated on all sides, then very carefully drop them into the hot fat. Fry over medium heat for about 1 minute until golden-brown. Remove with a slotted spoon and drain on kitchen paper. Serve hot, accompanied by the sweet-sour-hot sauce.

Stuffed glutinous rice balls

Not difficult • Most occasions **Kao niaw sot sai**

Serves 4 to 6

150 g glutinous rice
400 g boned chicken breast
3 sprigs fresh coriander
30 g chives
1 egg yolk
1 heaped tbsp cornflour
3 tbsp fish sauce (nam plah)
1 tbsp sugar
½ tsp freshly ground black pepper
1 small carrot
½ sweet green pepper
½ sweet red pepper
1 bowl sweet-sour-hot sauce
(page 32)

Preparation time: 50 minutes
(plus 2 hours' soaking time and
45 minutes for the sauce)

850 kJ/200 calories per portion
(if serving 6)

1 Soak the glutinous rice in hot water for at least 2 hours. Finely chop the chicken. Wash and dry the coriander and chop finely. Wash and trim the chives and chop finely. Put the chopped chicken, coriander and chives in a bowl with the egg yolk, cornflour, fish sauce, sugar and pepper, and mix them all together.

2 Drain the rice well and spread it out on a large plate. Place a teaspoonful of the chicken mixture on the bed of rice then, with damp hands, shape the rice round the chicken mixture to make a ball about 2 cm in diameter. Repeat with the remaining chicken and rice.

3 Bring a large pan of water to the boil. Line a bamboo or metal steamer (*see last paragraph, page 13*) with aluminium foil. Brush the the foil with oil then, using a chopstick, carefully

pierce a few holes in the foil. Place the rice balls in the steamer about 1 cm apart. Cover and steam over high heat for about 5 minutes. Reduce the heat to medium and continue to steam for a further 15 minutes.

4 Meanwhile, prepare the vegetables for the garnish. Peel and finely shred the carrot. Wash the pepper halves, remove the ribs and seeds, then shred finely. Arrange the cooked rice balls on a serving dish and garnish with the shredded vegetables and, if you like, carved raw vegetables such as carrot flowers (*see page 97*). Serve with sweet-sour-hot sauce.

Note: For the best results, soak the rice overnight; the more water it absorbs, the softer it will be. Thais use banana leaves to line the steamer, which can also be used as a base to serve the rice balls on.

Chicken soup with lemon grass

Not difficult · Hot   **Tom kah gai**   *Serves 4*

2 stalks fresh lemon grass
5 cm piece fresh galangal
3 fresh kaffir lime leaves
250 g oyster or button mushrooms
2 medium-sized tomatoes
3 fresh bird's-eye chili peppers
(see Glossary)
500 g boned chicken breasts
1 can (40 cl) unsweetened coconut
milk (see page 135)
fresh coriander
4 tbsp lime juice
4 tbsp fish sauce (nam plah)

Preparation time: 45 minutes

680 kJ/160 calories per portion

1 Wash the lemon grass and cut into 3 cm lengths. Peel and thinly slice the galangal. Wash the kaffir lime leaves and pat dry.

2 Trim the mushrooms, rinse briefly under running water, then cut them into bite-sized pieces (the smaller mushrooms can be left whole). Wash the tomatoes, quarter and core them. Wash the chilies, remove the stalks, then cut them into thin rings. Cut the chicken breasts into little strips about 1 cm wide and 4 cm long.

3 Heat the coconut milk in a pan. Add the lemon grass, lime leaves and sliced galangal. Cook over medium heat for about 2 minutes. Add ¾ litre water,

heat through, then add the chicken, mushrooms and tomatoes. Simmer the soup over low heat for about 5 minutes. At this stage, if you prefer, you can remove the lemon grass and galangal (the galangal is not eaten, the lemon grass could be eaten). Wash and dry the coriander and tear off the leaves.

4 Place the chilies, lime juice and fish sauce in a serving bowl. Pour in the hot soup, garnish with the coriander leaves and serve.

Note: If fresh kaffir lime leaves are unavailable, you can substitute dried ones; in which case you may prefer to remove them before serving the soup.

Galangal

Galangal, also known as Thai ginger, is one of the most important flavourings in Thai cuisine, where it is an indispensable ingredient in many soups and curries. Famed for its healing properties, it is said to help respiratory infections and stomach upsets and to aid digestion. In Thailand, grated galangal is often mixed with lime juice and taken as a tonic.

Similar in appearance to its more familiar relative, ginger, the galangal rhizome is larger and pale yellow in colour, with distinctive pink tips. It is highly aromatic and has a more

delicate flavour than ginger, with a sweetish, slightly medicinal taste.

Galangal is available all year round and can generally be found in Asian food shops. Always buy fresh, plump roots and use them as soon as possible—they will keep for about a

week in a cool place. Galangal can also be frozen, allowing you to break off pieces as needed. If fresh galangal is not available, use a smaller amount of fresh young ginger—although the flavour will be slightly different.

Noodle soup with red meat

Guay tiaw nahm moo daeng

More complex • Special occasions

Serves 4 to 6

3 to 4 sprigs fresh coriander
1 tsp freshly ground black pepper
2 tbsp tomato ketchup
2 tbsp sugar
2 tbsp fish sauce (nam plah)
few drops red food colouring
3 garlic cloves
1 tbsp vegetable oil
500 g pork fillet
150 g rice noodles
200 g bean sprouts
1.5 litres beef stock

For seasoning:
little bowls of chili powder, sugar,
chopped peanuts and
rice or other vinegar

Preparation time: 1 hour
(plus 2 hours' marinating time)

2,000 kJ/480 calories per portion
(if serving 6)

1 Wash the coriander and shake dry. Tear off the leaves and reserve. (To keep them fresh, put them in a sealed plastic bag.) Pound the stalks and the black pepper with a pestle and mortar, then transfer to a bowl and stir in the tomato ketchup, sugar, fish sauce and food colouring. Set aside. Peel and finely chop the garlic. Heat a little oil in a small frying pan and fry the garlic over medium heat for about 2 minutes until golden. Transfer to a plate.

2 Rinse the pork fillet under cold running water and pat dry. Trim off any skin and fatty membrane, then cut the fillet in half lengthwise. Prick both pieces at intervals with a fork. Coat with the ketchup marinade (*above*), cover, and leave to marinate in the refrigerator for at least 2 hours.

3 Preheat the oven to 200°C (400°F or Mark 6). Grease a large baking sheet. Lay the marinated meat on the baking sheet and sprinkle with the remaining oil. Roast in the centre of the oven for 15 to 20 minutes, depending on the thickness of the meat.

4 Meanwhile, cook the noodles in boiling water for about 3 minutes. Drain, and rinse briefly with cold water. Divide among individual soup bowls.

5 Bring a pan of water to the boil. Add the bean sprouts and blanch them for about 1 minute (*above*). Strain them through a sieve and divide them among the individual bowls containing the noodles.

6 Bring the stock to the boil. Remove the pork from the oven, carve it across the grain into slices about 5 mm thick (*above*) and divide the pieces among the individual bowls. Top up each bowl with hot stock, and sprinkle with the coriander leaves and fried garlic. Serve the soup accompanied by the little bowls of seasoning, so each person can season according to taste— for example, with a pinch of chili powder, about 1 tsp vinegar, 1 tsp sugar and 1 tsp chopped peanuts,

Note: Thais prefer to eat many dishes lukewarm rather than hot but if you prefer, you could put the bowls with the noodles and bean sprouts in the oven while you prepare the meat.

Fiery prawn soup

Fairly easy • Hot and aromatic   **Tom yam gung**   *Serves 4*

500 g medium-sized raw prawns
1 stalk fresh coriander with root
½ tsp black peppercorns
300 g button mushrooms
3 kaffir lime leaves
2 stalks fresh lemon grass
5 cm piece fresh galangal
4 fresh bird's-eye chili peppers
(see Glossary)
4 tbsp lime juice
4 tbsp fish sauce (nam plah)

Preparation time: 30 minutes

550 kJ/130 calories per portion

1 Shell the prawns, leaving the tails on, and reserve the heads and shells. Remove the dark, vein-like intestines.

2 Put the prawn heads and shells in a large pan, add 1.5 litres water and bring to the boil. Wash the coriander, cut off the root, trim and chop coarsely; reserve the leaves. Put the chopped root and the peppercorns in a mortar and pound with a pestle, or grind them in a food processor. Add them to the prawn stock and cook over medium heat for 5 to 10 minutes. Strain through a fine sieve into another pan.

3 Trim the mushrooms, rinse briefly under cold running water and cut the larger ones in half. Wash the lime leaves and lemon grass. Tear the leaves into quarters, cut the lemon grass into 3 cm lengths and lightly crush both with a knife. Peel and thinly slice the galangal.

4 Wash the chilies, discard the stalks and cut into thin rings. Mix them with the lime juice and fish sauce in a small bowl and set aside.

5 Boil the prawn stock with the lemon grass, lime leaves and galangal for about 2 minutes over medium heat. Add the prawns and the mushrooms, cover, and simmer over low heat for about 3 minutes. At this stage, you could remove the galangal (which should not be eaten) and, if you like, the lemon grass and lime leaves (which can be eaten if you wish).

6 Stir the chili and lime juice mixture into the soup. Transfer the soup to a serving bowl or individual soup bowls and serve, garnished with the reserved coriander leaves.

Fish soup with coconut milk

Tom plah gati sot

Not difficult • Southern Thailand

Serves 4 to 6

500 g fillet of coley, cod or redfish
6 tbsp fish sauce (nam plah)
½ tsp freshly ground black pepper
2 stalks fresh lemon grass
6 kaffir lime leaves
1 5 cm piece fresh galangal
3 sprigs fresh coriander
5 fresh bird's-eye chili peppers (see Glossary)
2 cans (40 cl each) unsweetened coconut milk (see page 135)
4 tbsp lime juice

Preparation time: 40 minutes

630 kJ/150 calories per portion (if serving 6)

1 Rinse the fish under cold running water, pat dry and cut into bite-sized pieces. Mix the pieces with 2 tbsp of the fish sauce and the pepper. Cover and leave to marinate in the refrigerator for about 20 minutes.

2 Meanwhile, wash the lemon grass and lime leaves. Cut the lemon grass into 3 cm lengths, tear the leaves into quarters. Peel and thinly slice the galangal. Wash and dry the coriander, remove the roots and finely chop the leaves. Wash the chilies, remove the stalks and cut into thin rings.

3 Pour the coconut milk into a pan and bring to the boil with the lemon grass, galangal and lime leaves. Add

the marinated fish pieces and the remaining fish sauce and cook over medium heat for about 2 minutes. Transfer to a bowl and add the lime juice, chopped chilies and coriander leaves. Stir thoroughly.

4 Remove the galangal (which should not be eaten) and, if you prefer, the lemon grass and lime leaves.

Variation: 300 g trimmed and washed oyster mushrooms, cut into bite-sized pieces, can be added to the soup at the same time as the fish.

Beef soup with chilies

Not difficult • Hot and aromatic　**Tom saeb neua**　*Serves 4 to 6*

2 stalks fresh lemon grass
6 kaffir lime leaves
5 cm piece fresh galangal
500 g boned shoulder of beef
6 fresh bird's-eye chili peppers (see Glossary)
50 holy, or other, basil leaves (see page 71)
300 g button mushrooms
2 medium-sized tomatoes
5 tbsp fish sauce (nam plah)
4 tbsp lime juice
½ tsp chili powder

Preparation time: about 30 minutes (plus 1¼ hours' simmering time)

620 kJ/150 calories per portion (if serving 6)

1 Wash the lemon grass and lime leaves. Cut the lemon grass into 3 cm lengths and tear the lime leaves into quarters. Peel and thinly slice the galangal.

2 Rinse the beef briefly under cold running water. Remove any fatty membranes and cut into bite-sized pieces. Bring 1.5 litres water to the boil in a pan, with the meat, lemon grass, galangal and lime leaves. Half cover the pan and simmer over medium heat for about 1¼ hours.

3 Wash the chili peppers, discarding the stalks, then place them on a chopping board and crush with a heavy knife. Wash the basil leaves, shake dry and set aside. Trim the mushrooms, rinse briefly under cold water and cut into quarters. Wash the tomatoes, remove the hard core under the stalks and cut into quarters.

4 When the meat is tender, add the mushrooms, tomatoes and fish sauce and continue to cook over medium heat for about 2 minutes. Pour the soup into a serving bowl and stir in the lime juice, crushed chili peppers, chili powder and basil leaves. Serve immediately.

Note: To reduce the hotness, you can halve the chilies and remove the seeds before crushing (*Step 3*).

Kaffir lime leaves and lemon grass

The shiny, dark green leaves of the kaffir lime tree and the rind of its ugly, knobbly fruit lend a distinctive lemony flavour to many Thai dishes. Used like bay leaves, these aromatic leaves are either added to the pan at the start of cooking, or cut into strips and used as a garnish.

Another indispensable flavour in Thai cuisine is lemon grass. Resembling a large spring onion, its thick, fibrous stalks give off a strong but subtle lemon fragrance when crushed, hence its name. Only the base of the stalk is used; sliced or shredded, it is added to soups, pastes and stuffings. Dried lemon grass is a common ingredient in herbal teas and is also used in Thai medicine to treat colds and aches in the stomach.

Both lemon grass and kaffir lime leaves can be found in Asian food shops. Fresh, they will keep for several weeks wrapped in a plastic bag in the refrigerator and can also be frozen. An approximate substitute for lemon grass, if unavailable, is lemon peel with a little grated ginger.

Hot prawn and tamarind soup

More complex • Bangkok

Gaeng som tua fak yao

Serves 4 to 6

6 large dried chili peppers (see Glossary)
3 shallots
3 fresh krachai roots (Chinese keys)
1 tsp salt
1 tsp shrimp paste
2 walnut-sized pieces compressed tamarind pulp
400 g medium-sized raw prawns
300 g Chinese long beans, or French beans
3 tbsp fish sauce (nam plah)
2 tbsp palm sugar (or, if unavailable, soft brown sugar)

Preparation time: 45 minutes

390 kJ/93 calories per portion (if serving 6)

1 Halve the chili peppers crosswise and soak in lukewarm water for about 5 minutes. Peel and finely chop the shallots. Wash or peel the *krachai* roots and cut into thin rings. Remove the chilies from the water and squeeze out the excess moisture, then crush in a mortar with the salt. Add the shrimp paste, shallots and *krachai* and carefully grind to a paste.

2 Place the tamarind pulp in a small bowl, cover with lukewarm water and soak for about 10 minutes, then knead thoroughly to produce a thick juice. Discard any hard bits or seeds, then strain through a very fine sieve.

3 Shell the prawns, leaving the tails on, and remove the dark, vein-like intestines. Trim and wash the beans and cut them into 4 cm lengths. Bring 1.5 litres water to the boil in a pan. Add the chili paste, fish sauce, palm

sugar, 3 tbsp tamarind juice and the beans, then simmer for about 3 minutes. Add the prawns and simmer for a further 2 minutes. Season with palm sugar and tamarind juice to the required sweet and sour flavour.

Variation: Instead of beans, you could use another vegetable, such as white radish (mooli) or Chinese cabbage.

Note: *Krachai*, or Chinese keys, is a type of ginger, similar in flavour to its close relative galangal (*see page 52*) but with a strong ginger-lemony aroma. The English name probably refers to the shape—a knobbly head with many finger-like roots hanging from it, rather like a bunch of keys. If you cannot find fresh *krachai* roots, use dried ones.

Be very careful when grinding chili paste; to avoid any juice squirting in your eyes, hold the pestle in one hand and shield the mortar with the other.

Stuffed cucumber soup

Tom jeut taeng gwah

Fairly easy • Most occasions

Serves 4

3 stalks fresh coriander with roots
15 garlic cloves
1½ tsp freshly ground black pepper
1 tsp salt
2 tbsp light soy sauce
150 g minced pork
150 g minced beef
4 tbsp vegetable oil
1 large cucumber
3 tbsp fish sauce (nam plah)
8 toothpicks

Preparation time: 50 minutes

1,200 kJ/290 calories per portion

1 Wash and shake dry the coriander. Finely chop the roots, coarsely chop the stalks and leaves and set aside. Peel the garlic. Put the coriander roots and 5 of the garlic cloves in a mortar with the pepper and salt and pound to a paste. Stir half this paste and the soy sauce into the minced meat, then cover and leave to marinate in the refrigerator for about 15 minutes.

2 Meanwhile, finely chop the rest of the garlic cloves. Heat the oil in a frying pan over medium heat and fry the chopped garlic for about 3 minutes until golden. Remove and reserve.

3 Peel the cucumber and cut it into four pieces. Remove the seeds using, for example, a spoon handle. Stuff with the minced meat. Insert a toothpick across the openings at either end of each stuffed section, to secure the filling.

4 Fill a pan with 1 litre water, add the remaining garlic and coriander paste and the fish sauce, and bring to the boil. Add the cucumber and cook, partially covered, over medium heat for about 7 minutes. Transfer to a serving bowl. Remove the toothpicks, add the chopped coriander, fried garlic and a little ground pepper and serve, accompanied, if you like, by plain, steamed fragrant rice (*page 82*).

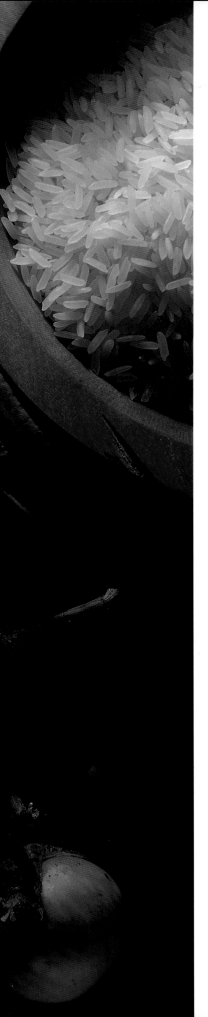

MEAT, RICE, NOODLES AND VEGETABLES

The staple of most Thai meals is fragrant rice. A large bowl of steaming fluffy rice is placed in the centre, surrounded by a variety of dishes including clear soups and different meats, seafood and vegetables combined with a range of spices and flavourings. Noodles—which most reflect the influence of Chinese cuisine—are a popular lunchtime snack, but they also feature in main meals, either as soups or fried dishes.

For meat and vegetable dishes, the ingredients are traditionally cut small, a technique derived from the old Thai habit—shared with India and Burma—of eating with the fingers of the right or "clean" hand; it also allows quick cooking and easy mixing with sauces and spices.

The meats vary according to the religion of the diners. Most Thais dislike lamb and mutton, preferring beef and pork, especially offal such as ears and trotters. However, the majority of the Hindus do not eat beef, and Muslims cannot eat pork. But Thailand provides a wonderful array of vegetables; and most meat dishes also include vegetables for contrasts of colour and flavour.

Much of the work of preparing many of these dishes, such as cutting up ingredients and flavourings, can be done well in advance. Cooking is usually a matter of the briefest stir-frying, to ensure freshness and crispness.

Beef with oyster sauce

Not difficult • Special occasions

Neua pat nam man hoy

Serves 4

500 g fillet of beef
½ tsp freshly ground black pepper
2 tbsp dark soy sauce • 1 tbsp flour
5 dried Chinese black mushrooms
300 g oyster mushrooms
2 spring onions
1 fresh jalapeño chili (see Glossary)
4 garlic cloves
1 walnut-sized piece fresh ginger root
3 tbsp vegetable oil
5 tbsp oyster sauce
1 tbsp fish sauce (nam plah)
1 tsp sugar • 4 tbsp rice wine (or medium-dry sherry)

Preparation time: 1¼ hours (including marinating time)

1,500 kJ/360 calories per portion

1 Rinse the beef under cold running water, pat dry and cut into 1 cm cubes, removing any fatty membrane. Mix with the pepper, soy sauce and flour. Cover and leave to marinate in the refrigerator for about 1 hour.

2 Soak the dried mushrooms in hot water for about 20 minutes.

3 Meanwhile, trim the oyster mushrooms, rinse briefly under running water, and chop coarsely. Trim and wash the spring onions, cut in half lengthwise, then again into 3 cm-long pieces. Wash the chili and cut it in half lengthwise. Remove the stalk and seeds and cut the flesh into strips. Peel and finely chop the garlic and the ginger.

4 Carefully squeeze the moisture from the dried mushrooms and cut them into quarters. Heat the oil in a wok or frying pan until sizzling hot. Stir-fry the garlic, ginger and beef over high heat for about 5 minutes until well browned. Reduce the heat and add both lots of mushrooms, the spring onions, oyster and fish sauces, and sugar. Cook over medium heat for about 2 minutes.

5 Add the chili pepper strips, cook briefly, then stir in the rice wine and serve immediately.

Beef curry

Takes a little time • Southern Thailand

Gaeng massaman

Serves 4

500 g rump or leg of beef
1 can (40 cl) unsweetened coconut milk (see page 135)
3 tbsp Massaman curry paste (page 28)
4 tbsp palm sugar or soft brown sugar
4 tbsp fish sauce (nam plah)
2 tbsp lime juice
3 tbsp salted, roasted peanuts
2 bay leaves
2 medium-sized onions
4 medium-sized waxy potatoes

Preparation time: 1¾ hours (plus 25 minutes for the curry paste)

1,500 kJ/360 calories per portion

1 Rinse the meat under cold running water, pat dry and cut into 2 cm cubes, removing any fatty membrane.

2 Skim 5 tbsp cream from the top of the coconut milk (*see Note, below*) into a large pan and bring it to the boil. Stir in the curry paste and continue to cook for about 1 minute. Add the beef, sugar, fish sauce, lime juice, peanuts, bay leaves, the rest of the coconut milk and ½ litre water.

3 Simmer, half covered, over low heat, for about 50 minutes. Peel and halve the onions. Peel and quarter the potatoes. Add the onions and potatoes to the pan and continue to simmer gently for a further 20 minutes.

4 Remove the bay leaves and serve immediately.

Variation: 750 g chicken breasts or thighs can be substituted for the beef; reduce the total cooking time to 50 minutes.

Note: To make sure that cream has formed on the top of the coconut milk, leave it in the refrigerator until you are ready to use it, then remember not to shake it up when opening the can.

Beef with green peppercorns
Pat neua prik thai orn

Serves 4

500 g fillet of beef
2 tbsp light soy sauce
1 tsp freshly ground black pepper
1 sweet red pepper
150 g fresh green peppercorns on the stalk
5 tbsp vegetable oil
2 tbsp red curry paste (page 26)
3 tbsp fish sauce (nam plah)
2 tbsp sugar

**Preparation time: 30 minutes
(plus 25 minutes for the curry paste)**

1,200 kJ/290 calories per portion

1 Wash the beef briefly under cold running water, pat dry and remove any fatty membrane. Cut into strips about 4 cm long and 1 cm wide. Mix with the soy sauce and ground black pepper. Cover and leave to marinate in the refrigerator for about 15 minutes.

2 Wash the sweet pepper, cut in half and remove the stalk, ribs and seeds. Cut each half in half again, then into strips. Carefully rinse the stalks of green peppercorns, then cut into 3 cm lengths.

3 Heat the oil in a wok or frying pan over medium heat. Add the red curry paste and fry it briefly. Add the beef, green peppercorns, sweet pepper strips, fish sauce, sugar and a little water. Stir-fry over medium heat for about 3 minutes.

Note: To tone down the fieriness of this curry, garnish it with 2 tbsp coconut cream (*see page 135*). If, however, you like it to taste even hotter, serve it with a bowl of chilies in vinegar (*page 32*).

Beef with green beans

Fairly easy • Hot and spicy   **Pat pet tua fak yao**   *Serves 4 to 6*

400 g rump steak
2 tbsp light soy sauce
½ tsp freshly ground black pepper
5 tbsp dried shrimps
5 kaffir lime leaves
300 g Chinese long beans or French beans
5 tbsp vegetable oil
2 tbsp red curry paste (page 26)
2 tbsp fish sauce (nam plah)
3 tbsp sugar

Preparation time: 30 minutes
(plus 25 minutes for the curry paste)

1,100 kJ/260 calories per portion
(if serving 6)

1 Wash the beef under cold running water and pat dry. Remove any fatty membrane and cut the meat across the grain into strips about 4 cm long by 1 cm wide. Mix with the soy sauce and pepper, cover and leave to marinate in the refrigerator for about 15 minutes. Crush the dried shrimps with a pestle and mortar—or grind them in a food processor—and set aside.

2 Wash the lime leaves, roll them up lengthwise and shred finely. Wash and trim the beans and cut into 4 cm lengths. Bring 1 litre water to the boil in a large pan. Blanch the beans for about 1 minute, then strain, and rinse under cold running water.

3 Heat the oil in a wok or frying pan until sizzling. Fry the beef for about 2 minutes until well browned. Reduce the heat, add the curry paste, crushed shrimps, beans, fish sauce and sugar and continue to fry over medium heat for about 4 minutes, stirring occasionally. Arrange on a serving dish, sprinkle with the shredded lime leaves and serve.

Variation: Strips of pork or chicken breast can be prepared in the same way. For added decorative effect, cut the beans into 8 cm lengths, blanch them as above, leave to cool, then knot carefully (*see photograph, page 96*).

Yellow beef curry

Gaeng garee neua

600 g rump or leg of beef
15 shallots
1 can (40 cl) unsweetened coconut
milk (see page 135)
2 tbsp yellow curry paste
(page 28)
3 tbsp fish sauce (nam plah)
160 g sugar
4 medium-sized waxy potatoes
1 cucumber
1 fresh red jalapeño chili pepper or
pimiento (see Glossary)
1 tsp salt
12.5 cl rice vinegar, or mild wine
vinegar
10 tbsp vegetable oil

Preparation time: 2 hours
(plus 25 minutes for the curry paste)

2,000 kJ/480 calories per portion
(if serving 6)

1 Wash the beef under cold running water and pat dry. Cut the meat (*above*) into 2 cm cubes. Trim, halve and slice the shallots and set aside.

2 Skim 4 tbsp cream from the top of the coconut milk (*see Note, page 64*) and bring it to the boil in a pan. Stir in the curry paste, reduce the heat to low and simmer for about 2 minutes. Add the cubes of beef, increase the heat, then gradually stir in the remaining coconut milk and ½ litre water.

3 Add the fish sauce and 1 tbsp of the sugar, then simmer over low heat, half covered, for about 50 minutes. Peel the potatoes, cut them into 2 cm cubes and add them to the pan. Continue to simmer for a further 15 to 20 minutes.

4 Meanwhile, to make the salad, peel or thoroughly wash the cucumber and cut it lengthwise into quarters, then slice thinly (*above*). Wash the chili pepper or pimiento, remove the stalk, and slice the flesh into thin rings. Place the slices of chili and cucumber in a bowl together with 3 tbsp of the sliced shallots. For the dressing, bring the salt, vinegar and remaining sugar to the boil in a small saucepan. Stir thoroughly, remove from the heat and allow to cool.

5 Heat the oil in a frying pan. Stir-fry the remaining sliced shallots over high heat until golden. Pour off the oil and reserve the fried shallots.

6 Mix the salad with the dressing. Place the beef curry in a serving bowl, sprinkle with the fried shallots and serve accompanied by a bowl of steamed fragrant rice (*page 82*).

Variation: Chicken joints can be substituted for the beef.

Green beef curry

Not difficult • Bangkok   **Gaeng kiaw wahn neua**   *Serves 4 to 6*

500 g fillet of beef
½ tsp salt
½ each fresh red and green jalapeño
chili peppers, or small pimientos
(see Glossary)
4 small green aubergines
(about 200 g)
50 basil (bai horapah) leaves
1 can (40 cl) unsweetened coconut
milk (see page 135)
2 tbsp green curry paste
(page 26)
4 tbsp fish sauce (nam plah)
3 tbsp palm sugar, or, if unavailable,
soft brown sugar

Preparation time: 30 minutes
(plus 25 minutes for the curry paste)

1 Wash the meat under cold running water, pat dry, then cut into fine strips about 4 cm long. Stir the salt into the meat. Wash the chili pepper or pimiento halves. Discard the stalks and seeds and cut into strips.

2 Wash the aubergines, cut them lengthwise into quarters and remove the stalks. (If using larger aubergines, cut them into 2 cm cubes.) Put them in a bowl, cover the aubergines with water and set aside. Wash the basil leaves and shake dry.

3 Skim 4 tbsp cream from the top of the coconut milk (*see Note, page 64*) into a pan and boil it for about 1 minute. Stir in the green curry paste.

Add the beef and the rest of the coconut milk. Fill the empty can about a quarter full with water. Swill it round to loosen any remaining coconut milk, then add it to the pan. Cook over medium heat for about 3 minutes.

4 Drain the aubergines. Add the chilies, aubergines, fish sauce and sugar to the pan and cook for a further 2 minutes. Stir in the basil and serve.

Variation: Instead of aubergines, use a 50 cl can of whole bamboo shoots. Rinse the bamboo shoots in cold water, drain, and cut into thin strips. The cooking time remains the same.

Note: If green aubergines are unavailable, you can substitute small white or purple ones.

70

Basil

This pungent herb, a native of India and long a popular ingredient in Mediterranean cooking, features prominently in Thai cuisine, where its leaves are used to flavour and garnish curries, salads, soups and stir-fried dishes.

Of the three varieties commonly used in Thailand, *bai horapah*, a tropical version of the familiar sweet basil, is the most popular. It has a smaller, darker leaf and reddish-purple stems and flowers. Its flavour—reminiscent of aniseed— is somewhat stronger than that of its European relation.

The highly aromatic *bai grapao*, or "holy" basil, was introduced to

Thailand by Indian Hindus. Its taste is hot and slightly medicinal. A third variety, *bai maenglak*, is characterized by its furry leaves. Wherever possible, use the specific type of basil called for in each recipe. However, the sweet Western variety may be used instead.

Good Asian food stores stock the Asian basil, but fresh sweet basil—

leaves and small plants—is readily available in most large supermarkets and greengrocers. Fresh basil will keep for a few days in the refrigerator if wrapped in damp kitchen paper or placed inside a plastic bag. During the warmer months, it can also be grown from seed in a pot or windowbox, but dislikes cold weather.

Pork satay

Moo satay

500 g pork fillet
about 40 wooden satay sticks or
skewers
2 cm piece fresh galangal
1 stalk fresh lemon grass
1 tsp coriander seeds
1 tsp cumin seeds
½ tsp salt
½ tsp freshly ground black pepper
100 g sugar
1 tbsp curry powder
1 can (40 cl) unsweetened coconut
milk (see page 135)
1 cucumber
5 shallots
1 fresh red jalapeño chili pepper
(see Glossary)
¼ litre rice vinegar, or mild
wine vinegar
1 bowl peanut sauce (page 35)

Preparation time: 1 hour
(plus 1 hour's marinating time and
25 minutes for the peanut sauce)

2,100 kJ/500 calories per portion

1 Wash the pork fillet in cold water and pat dry. Thinly slice the meat across the grain (*above*), then cut it into strips about 10 cm long and 3 cm wide. Soak the wooden satay sticks or skewers in water, to prevent them from charring during cooking.

2 Peel and finely chop the galangal. Wash, trim and thinly slice the lemon grass. In a mortar, or food processor, grind together the galangal, lemon grass, coriander and cumin seeds. Add the salt, pepper, 1 tbsp sugar, curry powder and 3 tbsp coconut cream (*see Note, page 64*). Stir the mixture into the meat, cover, and leave to marinate in the refrigerator for at least 1 hour.

3 Light a charcoal or ordinary grill, or preheat the oven to 250°C (475°F or Mark 9). Thread a piece of meat onto each satay stick or skewer concertina-wise—piercing in and out along the length (*above*). Leave one end free so the stick can be held without burning.

4 Thoroughly wash, or peel, the cucumber, cut into quarters lengthwise, then slice it thinly (*above*). Peel and thinly slice the shallots. Wash the chili pepper, remove the stalk and seeds, and cut the flesh into thin rings. Mix the cucumber, chili and shallots.

5 For the dressing, mix 12.5 cl water with the vinegar, the remaining sugar and a pinch of salt. Boil for about 1 minute, then leave to cool.

6 Toss the salad in the cold dressing, then sprinkle with a little additional vinegar and sugar to give it that extra sweet-and-sour flavour.

7 Grill the satays for about 3 minutes on each side, or cook at the top of the oven for about 15 minutes, turning once or twice, until browned. Serve with a bowl of slightly warmed peanut sauce and the salad.

Variation: You can also use strips of beef or chicken breast for this recipe.

Note: Ready-made satay mix and peanut sauce can be bought in Oriental food shops.

Pork fillet with pineapple

Not difficult • Special occasions

Moo op sapparot

Serves 4 to 6

4 large 1 cm thick slices fresh , or canned, pineapple
10 tbsp fresh, or canned, unsweetened pineapple juice
800 g pork fillet
1 tsp salt
½ tsp freshly ground black pepper
1 tbsp flour
1 tbsp sweet soy sauce
2 tbsp brown sugar
2 tbsp rice vinegar, or mild wine vinegar
3 tbsp vegetable oil
2 bay leaves
iceberg lettuce leaves
2 tomatoes

Preparation time: 30 minutes (plus 1 hour's marinating time)

1,500 kJ/360 calories per portion (if serving 6)

1 If using fresh pineapple, peel and core the slices. Wash the pork fillet under cold running water and pat dry. Remove any skin and fatty membrane, then cut the meat across the grain into 1 cm thick slices. Beat lightly with a meat tenderizer, then mix with the salt, pepper, flour, soy sauce, sugar, vinegar and pineapple juice. Cover and leave to marinate in the refrigerator for about 1 hour.

2 Heat the oil in a wok or frying pan. Place the meat in the pan and pour over the marinade. Add the bay leaves. Cover and cook over medium heat for about 3 minutes. Turn the meat and add the pineapple slices. Continue to cook, uncovered, for a further 3 minutes, stirring occasionally, until the pan juices thicken.

3 Wash the lettuce leaves and shake them dry. Wash the tomatoes and cut into quarters.

4 Carefully take the pineapple slices out of the pan and lay them on a serving dish. Arrange the slices of meat on top of the pineapple, garnish with the lettuce leaves and tomato wedges, and serve.

Variation: This recipe works equally well with beef fillet; preparation and cooking times are the same as for pork. Chili sauce with coriander (*page 30*) is a good accompaniment to this dish.

Sweet-and-sour meatballs

Pat priaw wahn look chin sapparot

Needs care • Most occasions

Serves 4 to 6

5 garlic cloves
½ tsp freshly ground black pepper
1 tsp salt
250 g finely minced pork
250 g finely minced beef
1 small fresh pineapple
½ sweet red pepper
½ sweet green pepper
3 tbsp fish sauce (nam plah)
2 tbsp rice vinegar, or mild wine vinegar
3 tbsp sugar
1 tsp cornflour
10 tbsp vegetable oil

Preparation time: 45 minutes

1,800 kJ/430 calories per portion (if serving 6)

1 Peel the garlic, then crush in a mortar together with the pepper and salt to form a paste. Knead the paste thoroughly with the minced pork and beef, then shape into about 25 smooth balls 2 cm in diameter, making sure there are no cracks in the surface.

2 Trim and cut the peel off the pineapple, removing the brown eyes. Quarter it lengthwise, remove the hard core, then thinly slice crosswise. Wash the sweet pepper halves and remove the ribs and seeds. Cut the flesh into 2 cm squares. To make the sauce, mix the fish sauce, rice vinegar, sugar, cornflour and 5 tbsp water in a small bowl until smooth.

3 Heat the oil in a wok or large frying pan. Fry the meatballs over medium heat for about 3 minutes until browned all over. Pour off any excess oil, add the pineapple and pepper strips, and cook for about 1 minute over high heat, until heated through. Add the prepared sauce and bring briefly to the boil, stirring carefully to coat the meatballs in the sauce.

Note: To prevent the meatballs from falling apart while frying, use meat that has been as finely minced as possible. If necessary, chop the mince once more before using it.

Pork with bamboo shoots

Not difficult • Spicy   **Pat pet moo sai nor mai**   *Serves 4 to 6*

400 g pork leg or fillet
3 tbsp fish sauce (nam plah)
½ tsp freshly ground black pepper
1 can (50 cl) bamboo shoots
½ sweet red pepper
½ sweet green pepper
5 tbsp vegetable oil
2 tbsp yellow curry paste (page 28)
2 tbsp sugar

Preparation time: 30 minutes
(plus 25 minutes for the curry paste)

1,200 kJ/290 calories per portion
(if serving 6)

1 Wash the meat under cold running water and pat dry. Cut it into strips about 1 cm wide and 4 cm long. Mix with 1 tbsp of the fish sauce and the ground pepper, and leave to marinate for about 10 minutes.

2 Meanwhile, drain the bamboo shoots, rinse them under cold running water and cut into thin strips. Wash the sweet pepper halves, remove the stalk, ribs and seeds, then cut them into thin strips.

3 Heat the oil in a wok or frying pan over medium heat. Fry the pork strips for about 2 minutes. Add the curry

paste and stir well. Increase the heat to high. Add the bamboo shoots, sweet peppers, the remainder of the fish sauce, sugar and a little water, and stir-fry for a further 2 minutes. Serve immediately.

Variation: Chicken breast or beef fillet can be used instead of the pork.

Bamboo shoots

Species of the tall, grasslike bamboo plant flourish throughout Southeast Asia. The cylindrical pointed shoots are harvested in the spring when they are 15 to 20 cm long. Beneath their brownish-black skin, which is shaved off before cooking, is a tender, yellowish flesh whose savoury sweetness and crunchy texture is a popular ingredient in Oriental cuisine.

Fresh bamboo shoots can occasionally be found in Asian or Chinese food stores. However, the shoots, once cut, develop an acrid flavour and pungent smell that renders them impossible to use

without lengthy boiling first. Good quality canned shoots, known as winter bamboo, are more convenient to use and are widely available—whole shoots being generally crisper and of better quality than those cut into slices. Before using canned shoots, first drain

them then rinse well in cold water.

If you do not need to use a whole can at once, transfer the remainder to a glass or plastic container, cover with water and refrigerate. If the water is changed every two days, the shoots will keep for a week or more.

Fried rice with prawns

Not difficult • Most occasions   **Kao pat gung**   *Serves 4*

500 g medium-sized raw prawns
2 tbsp light soy sauce
½ tsp freshly ground black pepper
2 medium-sized onions
2 spring onions
3 garlic cloves
1 cucumber
5 tbsp vegetable oil
750 g cold, cooked Thai fragrant rice (from 250 g uncooked rice, see page 82)
about 3½ tbsp fish sauce (nam plah)
2 tbsp tomato ketchup
1 tsp sugar

Preparation time: 40 minutes (plus 25 minutes for cooking the rice)

1,900 kJ/450 calories per portion

1 Wash and shell the prawns, leaving the tails on, and remove the dark, vein-like intestines. Mix the soy sauce and pepper, coat the prawns with the mixture, and leave to marinate for about 10 minutes.

2 Meanwhile, trim and peel the onions and slice into thin rings. Trim and wash the spring onions, halve lengthwise, then cut them into 3 cm-long pieces. Peel and finely chop the garlic. Wash the cucumber thoroughly, and cut it into slices about 5 mm thick.

3 Heat the oil in a wok or large frying pan. Fry the garlic over medium heat for about 2 minutes until golden. Add the prawns and stir-fry over high heat until they turn pale red. Add the onion rings and continue stir-frying for a further minute.

4 Add the rice, spring onions, 3 tbsp of the fish sauce, the tomato ketchup and sugar to the pan, and cook over high heat for a further 2 minutes, stirring from time to time, until everything is very hot. Season with a little more fish sauce. Serve on individual plates, garnished with the slices of cucumber.

Variation: Instead of the prawns, you could use 300 g pork escalope or boned chicken breast, cut into thin strips.

Three-friends curry

Not difficult • Fairly hot   **Gaeng pet trai mit**   *Serves 4 to 6*

200 g boned leg of pork
200 g rump steak
200 g boned chicken breast
1 can (40 cl) unsweetened coconut milk (see page 135)
2 tbsp Massaman curry paste (page 28)
4 cm piece fresh ginger root
2 heads pickled garlic (page 35)
4 tbsp fish sauce (nam plah)
3 tbsp palm sugar (or, if unavailable, soft brown sugar)

Preparation time: 1 hour (plus 25 minutes for the curry paste)

880 kJ/210 calories per portion (if serving 6)

1 Cut the pork, beef and chicken breast across the grain into strips about 1 cm wide and 4 cm long, keeping them in separate piles.

2 Skim 4 tbsp cream off the top of the coconut milk (*see Note, page 64*), bring it to the boil in a pan, then cook over medium heat for about 1 minute. Add the curry paste and stir thoroughly. Add the beef, 12.5 cl water and the remainder of the coconut milk. Cook, half-covered, over medium heat for about 30 minutes.

3 Peel the ginger and cut it into thin slivers. Peel and slice the pickled garlic. Set both aside.

4 Add the chicken and pork, fish sauce and sugar to the pot and cook over medium heat for about 10 minutes. Serve, sprinkled with the ginger and garlic.

Note: If you do not like garlic, 1 tbsp lemon juice added to the curry as it cooks will give a similar slightly sour flavour, without the taste of garlic.

Fried rice with seafood

More complex • Special occasions

Kao pat talay

500 g mixed seafood (prawns, cleaned squid, saltwater fish fillets)
8 garlic cloves
3 spring onions
2 medium-sized tomatoes
3 sprigs fresh coriander
1 cucumber
5 tbsp vegetable oil
750 g cold, cooked Thai fragrant rice (from 250 g uncooked rice, see page 82)
3 tbsp fish sauce (nam plah)
2 tbsp tomato ketchup
1 tsp sugar
1 bowl chili sauce with coriander (page 30)

Preparation time: 30 minutes (plus 25 minutes for cooking the rice, and 15 minutes for the chili sauce)

3,800 kJ/900 calories per portion

1 Wash the seafood and drain thoroughly. Shell the prawns, leaving the tails on and removing the dark, vein-like intestines. Cut the squid pouches into quarters, score the flesh crosswise and cut it into strips about 5 cm long and 2 cm wide. Cut the fish fillets into bite-sized pieces.

2 Peel and finely chop the garlic. Wash the spring onions, halve lengthwise, then cut into 3 cm-long pieces. Wash the tomatoes and cut into eighths. Wash the coriander, shake dry, and chop coarsely. Peel the cucumber and cut it into slices about 5 mm thick.

3 Heat the oil in a wok or large frying pan. Fry the garlic over medium heat for about 2 minutes, until golden. Add the seafood and toss over high heat for about 2 minutes. Add the rice, fish sauce, tomato ketchup, tomato wedges, spring onions and sugar, and stir-fry for a further 2 minutes.

4 Arrange on a serving dish, garnish with cucumber slices and sprinkle with coriander. Serve accompanied by the chili sauce with coriander.

Note: Fried rice dishes are a good way of using up leftover boiled rice. If using freshly cooked rice, allow it to cool thoroughly before frying; otherwise it will stick together. Mixed seafood can sometimes be bought ready to cook. If not, buy about 200 g of each, and clean as necessary.

Rice

Rice is both the staple and heart of Thai cuisine. An essential at every meal, its importance is reflected in the exhortation "*gin kao*", or "eat rice", that summons guests to table.

Rice is also a mainstay of Thailand's agriculture: across the country's fertile central plains region, watered by the Chao Phraya River, the grain is cultivated in such huge quantities that today Thailand is the world's leading exporter of rice. To a large extent, planting and harvesting—which take place two to three times a year—still dictate the life cycle of the rural population.

The preferred rice in central and southern Thailand is white, long-grain fragrant rice (*kao hom*). Readily available here from supermarkets as well as Asian stores, it is relatively expensive but has a superior flavour and a wonderful, refreshing jasmine aroma that is released as it cooks.

In north and northwest Thailand the staple rice is generally the starchy glutinous round-grain *kao niaw*, also known as sticky rice. Elsewhere in Thailand, glutinous rice tends to be used only for stuffings, puddings and sweet dishes. There are also other varieties, including a black glutinous rice, which has a nuttiness similar to wild rice and is used in desserts.

Thai fragrant rice

Basic recipe • Simple

Kao suay

Serves 4

250 g Thai fragrant rice (see page 81)

Preparation time: 25 minutes

910 kJ/220 calories per portion

1 Rinse the rice thoroughly under cold running water, then transfer to a large pan. Add enough water to reach about 2 cm above the surface of the rice.

2 Cover the pan and bring the water to the boil, then remove the lid and reduce the heat. When the rice begins to simmer gently, replace the lid and continue simmering over low heat for about 20 minutes, or until the rice is fluffy and has absorbed all the water.

Note: Though not strictly accurate, rice cooked this way is usually known as "steamed rice". If using it for a fried rice dish, leave it to stand uncovered in the pan until completely cooled.

Curried chicken rice

Not difficult • Southern Thailand

Kao pat pong garee

Serves 4

400 g boned chicken breasts
1 tbsp curry powder
4 tbsp fish sauce (nam plah)
3 medium-sized waxy potatoes
iceberg lettuce leaves
½ cucumber
5 shallots
8 tbsp vegetable oil
750 g cold, cooked Thai fragrant rice (from 250 g uncooked rice, see above)
2 tsp sugar
1 bowl chilies in vinegar (page 32)

Preparation time: 45 minutes (plus 25 minutes for cooking the rice)

2,100 kJ/500 calories per portion

1 Dice the chicken breasts into bite-sized pieces. Mix the curry powder with 1 tbsp fish sauce and stir it into the chicken. Cover and leave to marinate in the refrigerator for about 20 minutes.

2 Meanwhile, peel the potatoes and cut them into 2 cm cubes. Place them in a pan with water and cook for 10 to 15 minutes, or until tender but still firm; drain and reserve. Wash the lettuce leaves and shake dry. Wash and thinly slice the cucumber. Peel, halve and slice the shallots.

3 Heat the oil in a wok or large frying pan until sizzling. Briefly brown the shallots over high heat. Add the marinated chicken and the potatoes and stir-fry over high heat for about 2 minutes. Add the rice and the remainder of the fish sauce. Stir thoroughly and heat through over medium heat for about 2 minutes.

4 Arrange the lettuce leaves and cucumber slices on a serving dish, and place the chicken, potato and rice mixture on top. Stir the sugar into the chilies in vinegar. Serve the rice hot, accompanied by the chilies.

Variation: This dish works well with roast chicken joints. Marinate the chicken joints in the curry powder and fish sauce, then roast them in the centre of the oven at 190°C (375°F or Mark 5) for about 30 minutes before adding them to the pan in Step 3.

Rice noodles with squid

Fairly easy • Special occasions   **Guay tiaw plah-meuk**   *Serves 4*

500 g cleaned squid
200 g broccoli
5 garlic cloves
2 medium-sized onions
200 g rice noodles (1 to 2 cm wide)
8 tbsp vegetable oil
2 tbsp sweet soy sauce
3 tbsp fish sauce (nam plah)
1 tbsp sugar

To serve (optional):
1 bowl chilies in vinegar (page 32)
sugar and chili powder

Preparation time: 30 minutes

1,900 kJ/450 calories per portion

1 Wash the squid under cold running water, pat dry, and cut the pouches lengthwise into quarters. Score the flesh crosswise, then cut it into strips about 5 cm long and 2 cm wide.

2 Wash the broccoli and break into florets. Peel the stalks, discarding any woody bits, and slice thinly. Peel and finely chop the garlic. Peel and quarter the onions.

3 Bring plenty of water to the boil in a saucepan. Add the noodles and cook them for about 3 minutes. Strain, rinse under cold running water, then drain thoroughly. Heat the oil in a wok or large frying pan. Stir-fry the garlic, onions and squid over high heat for about 1 minute.

4 Add the broccoli, and continue to stir-fry for about 2 minutes. Add the noodles, soy sauce, fish sauce and sugar and stir until thoroughly heated through.

5 Serve, if you like, accompanied by chili peppers in vinegar, and small individual bowls of sugar and chili powder, so that guests can add their own seasoning.

Note: When preparing rice noodles for adding to a dish, do not allow them to become dry, otherwise they will not mix well with the other ingredients. It is therefore important to work quickly in Steps 3 and 4.

Egg noodles with bean sprouts

Quick and easy • Mild **Ba mee pat** *Serves 4*

300 g Chinese egg noodles
200 g bean sprouts
2 spring onions
3 garlic cloves
50 g lean bacon
3 tbsp vegetable oil
2 tbsp fish sauce (nam plah)
2 tbsp oyster sauce
1 tbsp sugar

Preparation time: 25 minutes

1,700 kJ/400 calories per portion

1 Bring plenty of water to the boil in a saucepan. Cook the noodles in the water for about 4 minutes (*see Note, below*). Strain, rinse briefly with cold water, and drain.

2 Wash the bean sprouts, removing any that are discoloured. Trim and wash the spring onions, cut in half lengthwise, then again into 3 cm-long pieces. Peel and finely chop the garlic. Dice the bacon.

3 Heat the oil in a wok or frying pan. Add the garlic and bacon and cook for about 1 minute. Add the noodles, stir thoroughly, and continue cooking for a further minute.

4 Add the bean sprouts, spring onions, fish sauce, oyster sauce and sugar. Stir-fry over medium heat for about 2 minutes until everything is thoroughly heated through—the bean sprouts should still be crisp. Serve at once.

Note: Chinese egg noodles cook more quickly than their Italian equivalents; so it is best to follow the approximate cooking times given on the package and check the noodles are done before you drain them.

Stir-fried noodles

Pat thai gung sot

400 g medium-sized raw prawns
½ tsp freshly ground black pepper
3 tbsp fish sauce (nam plah)
3 garlic cloves
5 shallots
100 g salted, roasted peanuts
500 g bean sprouts
3 large green leek leaves
2 limes
100 g fresh, or vacuum-packed, firm tofu
200 g thin rice noodles (5 mm wide)
6 tbsp vegetable oil
50 g dried shrimps
2 eggs
2 tbsp rice vinegar, or mild wine vinegar
2 tbsp sugar
2 tbsp light soy sauce

To serve:
chili powder
sugar
1 bowl chilies in vinegar (optional; page 32)

Preparation time: 1 hour

2,400 kJ/570 calories per portion

1 Wash and shell the prawns, leaving the tails on and removing the dark, vein-like intestines. Mix the prawns with the pepper and 1 tbsp fish sauce (*above*), and marinate for about 10 minutes. Peel and finely chop the garlic and the shallots. Coarsely crush the peanuts in a mortar, or grind them in a food processor.

2 Wash the bean sprouts, and set aside. Wash the leek leaves and cut them into strips 4 cm long and 5 mm wide. Wash the limes in hot water, and quarter them. Cut the tofu into 5 mm dice (*above*).

3 Bring plenty of water to the boil in a saucepan and cook the noodles for about 2 minutes. Strain, and rinse under cold water, then drain. Heat the oil in a wok and fry the garlic, shallots, tofu and dried shrimps over high heat for 1 to 2 minutes. Add the prawns and toss for about 1 minute, then push all the ingredients to the sides of the wok.

4 Break the eggs into the centre of the wok, stir and cook over medium heat for about 3 minutes until scrambled. Mix the eggs thoroughly with the other ingredients in the pan. Add the noodles, half the bean sprouts, leek, vinegar, sugar, the remaining fish sauce and the soy sauce (*above*). Stir in quickly, heat through and transfer to a serving dish. Sprinkle with the chopped peanuts and keep warm.

5 Blanch the remaining bean sprouts in boiling water for about 1 minute, then drain. Arrange the bean sprouts and the lime wedges in two small bowls. Serve the noodles with a small bowl each of chili powder and sugar, and, if you like, a bowl of chilies in vinegar. Stir-fried noodles should have a sweet-and-sour flavour.

Note: This dish is traditionally accompanied by banana flowers, the hearts of which are edible. Peel off the purple outer petals and cut the tender white inner petals lengthwise into eighths. To prevent them from turning black, put them in water with some lemon juice until ready to serve. Banana flowers produce stubborn stains, so be careful not to splash your clothes.

Minced beef salad

Lahp neua

Serves 4

3 tbsp glutinous rice
4 tbsp lime juice
500 g minced beef
10 shallots
2 cm piece fresh galangal
5 kaffir lime leaves
3 stalks fresh coriander
30 g chives
30 leaves fresh mint
4 tbsp fish sauce (nam plah)
2 tsp chili powder

Preparation time: 30 minutes

1,400 kJ/330 calories per portion

1 Dry-roast the glutinous rice in a heavy frying pan for about 3 minutes, until browned. Leave to cool, then crush finely using a pestle and mortar or a food processor.

2 Mix the lime juice with the minced beef, knead thoroughly, then leave to stand for about 5 minutes. Peel the shallots and cut them into rings. Peel and finely chop the galangal. Wash the lime leaves, shake dry, roll up lengthwise, then shred finely. Wash the coriander, shake dry and tear the sprigs off the stalks. Wash the chives, shake dry and chop finely. Wash the mint and shake dry.

3 Heat a wok or heavy-bottomed saucepan, and fry the minced beef, without oil, over medium heat for about 5 minutes. Add the fish sauce and the chili powder, and stir thoroughly.

Remove the pan from the heat and stir in the crushed rice, lime leaves, chives, coriander, galangal and shallots.

4 Transfer to a serving dish, garnish with the mint leaves and serve warm.

Variation: Minced pork, or a mixture of minced pork and beef, can be used in this recipe.

Note: It is the crushed, dry-roasted glutinous rice which gives this salad its characteristic aroma and makes the sauce creamy. Always use freshly roasted rice. Crispy raw vegetables such as white cabbage, Chinese cabbage or iceberg lettuce are an ideal accompaniment for this dish.

Beef salad with coriander

Yam neua

Not difficult • Bangkok

Serves 4

3 garlic cloves
5 fresh bird's-eye chili peppers
(see Glossary)
4 tbsp fish sauce (nam plah)
4 tbsp lime juice
1 tbsp sugar
2 medium-sized onions
30 g chives
1 stalk fresh coriander
500 g fillet of beef
2 tbsp vegetable oil

Preparation time: 50 minutes

1,100 kJ/260 calories per portion

1 Peel the garlic. Wash the chili peppers and remove the stalks. Crush the garlic and chilies to a paste in a mortar—or use a food processor—then transfer them to a bowl. Stir in the fish sauce, lime juice and sugar.

2 Peel the onions, halve them lengthwise, then slice finely. Wash the chives, shake dry and cut into 3 cm lengths. Wash the coriander, shake dry and chop coarsely.

3 Rinse the beef under cold running water and pat dry. Remove any skin or membrane and cut the meat into small steaks about 1 cm thick. Heat the oil in a wok or large frying pan

until sizzling, then fry the steaks over high heat for about 2 minutes on either side, or until medium-done. Allow the steaks to cool, then cut into thin strips.

4 Add the meat, onions, chives and coriander to the garlic, chili and fish sauce mixture, and stir thoroughly. Serve immediately.

Note: Fillet is expensive, but it is the most tender of all beef cuts, especially when well-hung and so best suited for such brief cooking.

Squid salad

Yam plah-meuk

Serves 4

2 medium-sized onions (1 red,
1 white)
3 garlic cloves
5 fresh bird's-eye chili peppers (see
Glossary)
1 stalk fresh coriander with root
3 tbsp fish sauce (nam plah)
3 tbsp lime juice
1 tsp sugar
500 g cleaned squid

Preparation time: 45 minutes

440 kJ/100 calories per portion

1 Peel the onions, halve lengthwise, and slice thinly. Peel the garlic. Wash the chili peppers and remove the stalks and seeds. Wash the coriander and shake dry. Cut off the root and set aside; finely chop the stalk and leaves.

2 Using a pestle and mortar, or food processor, crush the coriander root with the garlic and chili peppers. Transfer the mixture to a salad bowl. Add the fish sauce, lime juice and sugar, and stir thoroughly.

3 Rinse the squid under cold running water and cut the pouches lengthwise into quarters. Score the flesh

crosswise, then cut into strips about 5 cm long and 1 cm wide.

4 Bring some water to the boil in a pan. Blanch the squid in the boiling water for about 1 minute, then drain. Add the warm squid, onions and coriander to the sauce, and stir thoroughly. Serve warm.

Variation: You could substitute peeled prawns for 200 g of the squid. Cook the prawns for about 2 minutes before stirring them into the salad.

Piquant chicken salad

Lahp ok gai

Serves 4

2 tbsp uncooked glutinous rice
10 shallots
30 g chives
40 leaves fresh mint
500 g boned chicken breast
few lettuce leaves
2 tsp chili powder
4 tbsp fish sauce (nam plah)
1 tsp sugar
4 tbsp lime juice

Preparation time: 30 minutes

790 kJ/190 calories per portion

1 Dry-roast the glutinous rice in a frying pan over medium heat for about 3 minutes until browned. Leave to cool, then crush finely with a pestle and mortar or food processor.

2 Peel the shallots and slice thinly. Wash the chives, shake dry and chop finely. Wash the mint and shake dry. Set aside half the leaves and finely chop the remainder.

3 Bring about 1 litre water to the boil in a pan. Rinse the chicken breast, pat dry, then place in the water. Reduce the heat to low and simmer the chicken for 10 to 15 minutes, or until cooked

through. Remove from the pan, and with two forks tear the meat into small strips. Wash the lettuce leaves and shake dry.

4 Mix the chicken shreds with the crushed rice, shallots, chives, chopped mint, chili powder, fish sauce, sugar and lime juice. Serve, accompanied by a bowl of lettuce leaves—or, if you like, on a bed of lettuce—and garnished with the rest of the mint leaves.

Note: Raw, shredded, white cabbage or Chinese cabbage, and briefly blanched Chinese long beans, go well with this dish.

Papaya salad

Som tam thai

1 medium-sized green, unripe
papaya (about 500 g)
4 garlic cloves
5 fresh bird's-eye chili peppers (see
Glossary)
2 medium-sized tomatoes
50 g dried shrimps
50 g salted, roasted peanuts
3 tbsp fish sauce (nam plah)
3 tbsp sugar
4 tbsp lime juice

Preparation time: 30 minutes

690 kJ/160 calories per portion

1 Peel the papaya and cut it in half lengthwise. Scrape out the seeds with a spoon and discard. Rinse the two halves, then finely shred the flesh.

2 Peel the garlic, wash the chilies and remove the stalks. Wash the tomatoes and cut into eighths. Using a large pestle and mortar (*see Note*), grind the garlic and 4 chilies. Add the shrimps and peanuts and grind coarsely.

3 Add the papaya to the mortar a little at a time, and carefully crush with the pestle. As it is crushed, stir it into the other ingredients with a spoon held in your other hand. Add the tomatoes, fish sauce, sugar and lime juice. Bruise the tomatoes slightly and stir the mixture thoroughly.

4 Leaving one end whole, cut the remaining chili pepper lengthwise into 8 "petals". Pull back each section to make a flower shape. Transfer the salad to a serving dish and garnish it with the chili flower.

Note: Accompany this salad with cooked glutinous rice (*see Steps 1 and 2, top recipe, page 32*) and raw vegetables such as Chinese cabbage leaves, white cabbage or young spinach. If you do not have a large pestle and mortar, use a bowl and crush the shredded papaya with a wooden meat tenderizer and use a small pestle and mortar, or a blender, to grind the garlic, chili peppers and peanuts separately, then mix them into the salad.

Papaya

The papaya, or pawpaw, native to Mexico, has been cultivated since the 16th century throughout Southeast Asia. The long, pear-shaped fruits, which can grow to enormous size, have a leathery, greenish skin that turns yellow when ripe. Beneath the inedible peel is a fragrant, peachy coloured flesh with a flavour reminiscent of melon and a mass of shiny black seeds that resemble peppercorns.

Papayas are delicious eaten on their own—a dash of lime juice brings out the exquisite flavour—or in a fruit salad. Unripe papaya can be cooked and eaten as a vegetable; in Thailand, where they are in plentiful supply, the shredded, unripe green flesh is used as a refreshing salad ingredient. Papaya juice contains a powerful enzyme that acts as a meat tenderizer when added to a marinade.

Papayas are most readily available in spring and summer. Ripe fruit have yellowish, wrinkly skin; the flesh should also give slightly when pressed with the fingers. A ripe papaya will keep for about a week in a cool, humid place.

Stir-fried vegetables

Pat pak ruam mit

Simple, but takes time • Bangkok

Serves 4

200 g broccoli
150 g French beans
200 g baby sweetcorn
300 g small spring carrots
200 g Chinese cabbage
3 spring onions
5 garlic cloves
5 tbsp vegetable oil
3 tbsp fish sauce (nam plah)
3 tbsp oyster sauce
1 tbsp sugar
4 tbsp rice wine (or medium-dry sherry)

To serve (optional):
1 bowl chili sauce with coriander (page 30) or 1 bowl chilies in vinegar (page 32)

Preparation time: 40 minutes

820 kJ/200 calories per portion

1 Wash the broccoli and cut off the florets. Peel and thinly slice the stalks (*above*), discarding any woody bits. Top and tail the beans and cut them in half.

2 Trim the sweetcorn and cut them in half crosswise, halving again lengthwise any especially thick ones. Peel the carrots and quarter them lengthwise. Cut the quarters in half crosswise (*above*).

3 Trim the Chinese cabbage and chop into bite-sized pieces. Trim the spring onions, halve lengthwise, then cut into 3-cm long pieces. Keep the spring onions and Chinese cabbage separate: they will take less time to cook. Wash all the vegetables and drain thoroughly.

4 Peel and finely chop the garlic. Heat the oil in a wok or large frying pan. Fry the garlic over high heat for about 1 minute. Add the broccoli, carrots, beans and sweetcorn and stir-fry over high heat for about 2 minutes. Stir in the spring onions, cabbage, fish sauce, oyster sauce and sugar.

5 Add the rice wine, reduce the heat to medium and stir-fry for another minute, until the vegetables are cooked through but still crisp. Serve immediately, accompanied, if you like, by either chili sauce with coriander or chilies in vinegar.

Variation: Many other vegetables can be stir-fried in this way—green asparagus, spinach, mushrooms, celery, mange-touts and cauliflower are all suitable—but bear in mind that some vegetables take longer to cook than others.

Note: Stir-frying is a quick, easy and nutritious cooking method; small pieces of meat or fish cook very quickly in the heat of a wok, allowing vegetables to retain their colour and vitamins and stay crisp.

Vegetable platter with dip

Easy, but takes time • Spicy   **Pak jim nam prik**   *Serves 4 to 6*

100 g Chinese long beans, or
French beans
100 g white cabbage
100 g baby sweetcorn
100 g cauliflower
100 g Chinese cabbage
100 g carrots
100 g aubergines
100 g onions
150 g fresh spinach
5 eggs
½ tsp salt
3 tbsp vegetable oil

For serving:
1 bowl tomato and minced meat dip
(page 36)

Preparation time: 1 hour
plus 25 minutes for the dip)

1,900 kJ/450 calories per portion
(if serving 6)

1 Top and tail the beans. Cut the white cabbage into small wedges. Trim the sweetcorn and halve thick ones lengthwise. Break the cauliflower into bite-sized florets. Trim the Chinese cabbage and separate the leaves. Peel the carrots and halve lengthwise. Wash all the vegetables and drain well.

2 Bring a pan of water to the boil and cook—separately, if you prefer—the beans, carrots, sweetcorn, cauliflower, and the two cabbages for about 2 minutes. Drain and leave to cool. If using Chinese long beans, knot them, as illustrated below.

3 Wash the aubergines and cut them into slices about 5 mm thick. Peel the onions and slice into 5 mm-thick rings. Remove the stems from the spinach, wash, shake dry and chop coarsely.

4 Whisk the eggs with the salt in a bowl. Heat the oil in a frying pan over medium heat. Fry the onions and aubergines—dipped first, if you like, in the beaten eggs—in batches for about 2 minutes. Remove from the pan, drain on kitchen paper and keep warm. Mix the chopped spinach with the beaten eggs and fry in the pan for about 2 minutes on each side, until the eggs are set firm. Cut into diamond-shaped wedges.

5 Arrange all the vegetables on a large serving dish, and serve accompanied by the tomato and minced meat dip.

Note: The choice of vegetables and dips can be varied according to taste, and to what is in season.

Vegetable carving

A poem by the 19th-century Thai king Rama II tells the story of a queen driven from the royal court by a rival. Returning to the royal household disguised as a kitchen maid, the queen is able to attract the attention of her son by carving the pieces of pumpkin served to him into scenes depicting events in her life. Recognizing the hand behind the carvings, the son rescues his mother and restores her to the throne. This incident is traditionally held to be the origin of the ancient and highly cultivated Thai art of fruit and vegetable carving.

The Thais pay great attention to the presentation of their food; the simplest of dishes are garnished and the ugliest of vegetables transformed into bouquets of beautiful flowers. The Grand Palace in Bangkok still has its own Royal Carver, and there are associations of professional fruit and vegetable carvers.

The possibilities are endless and range from simple tomato roses, cucumber leaves and spring onion tassels to intricate garnishes such as tiny crabs fashioned from pieces of ginger. For festive occasions, fruit such as pineapples, watermelons and pumpkins are transformed into elaborately carved and pierced serving containers or sculptures involving hours of painstaking work.

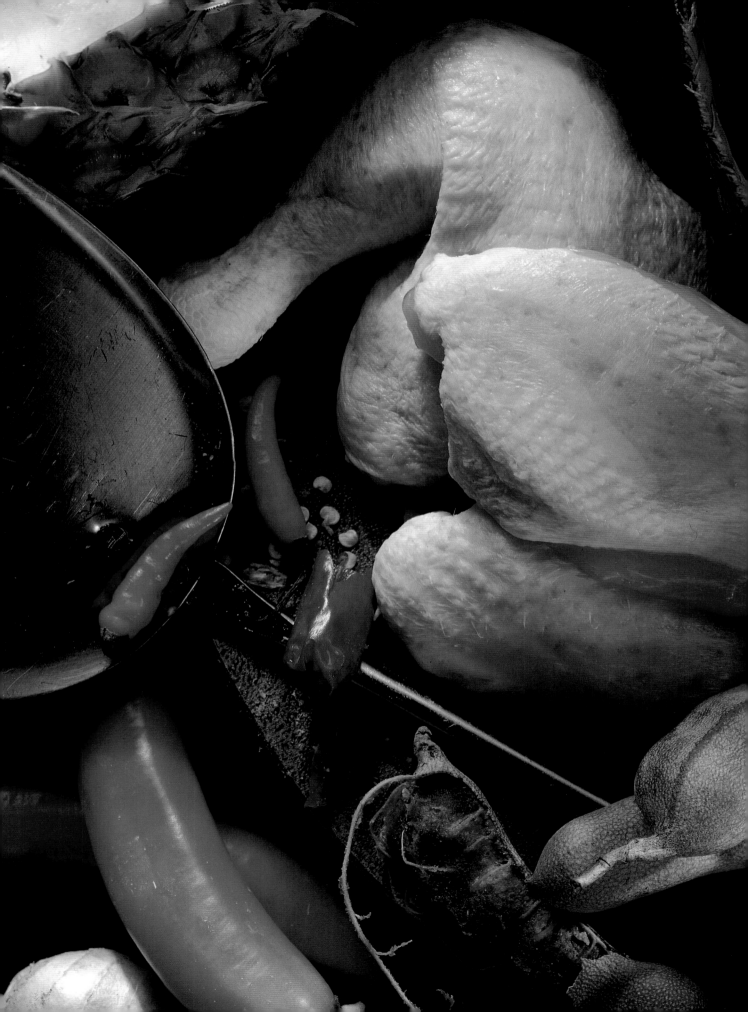

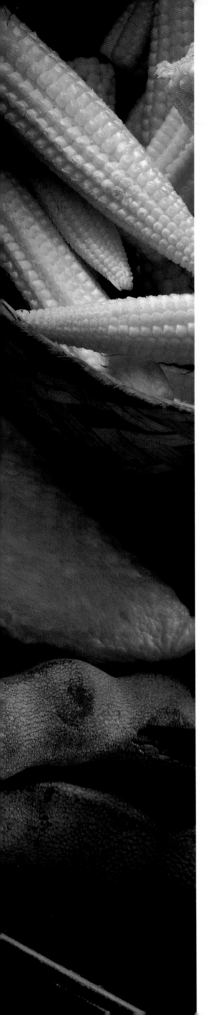

POULTRY DISHES

For most Thais, poultry is a source of protein second only to fish. Duck is a special treat for important occasions, but chicken is available everywhere. People indulging in *pai thiau*—a pleasant, aimless stroll—buy cooked chicken from street vendors, who serve grills and satays, as well as many other delicious snacks. And in the street food markets fresh chicken is sold for cooking at home in all sorts of forms—from whole, half or quarter birds to boneless breasts and ready-cut bite-sized pieces for satays.

As the recipes in this chapter show, the meat's mild flavour harmonizes with all kinds of fresh vegetables and fruits. It also mixes well with other meats, such as beef or pork, as in Three-friends curry (*page 78*), and with prawns or other seafood. It is the basis of many soups—for example, Chicken soup with lemon grass (*page 52*)—and is particularly delicious when served in one of the various curry sauces that are a speciality of Thailand (*page 105*).

And chicken has another advantage. The meat cooks quickly. With a little planning, stir-fried chicken dishes for guests can be prepared in a trice. When duck is served, it is often roasted, the meat removed from the bones and combined with a sauce as, for example, the tamarind sauce on page 112.

Chicken with pineapple

Ok gai sapparot

Not difficult • Sweetly refreshing

Serves 4 to 6

500 g boned chicken breasts
1 tbsp cornflour
2 tbsp light soy sauce
½ tsp freshly ground black pepper
1 sweet red pepper
1 sweet green pepper
1 medium-sized carrot
1 small, fresh pineapple
5 tbsp vegetable oil
3 tbsp fish sauce (nam plah)
2 tbsp sugar
3 tbsp rice wine (or, if unavailable, medium-dry sherry)

Preparation time: 35 minutes (including marinating time)

950 kJ/230 calories per portion (if serving 6)

1 Rinse the chicken, pat dry and cut into 2 cm dice. In a bowl, mix the cornflour, soy sauce and pepper. Stir in the chicken, cover and leave to marinate in the refrigerator for about 20 minutes.

2 Meanwhile, wash the sweet peppers. Cut in half, remove the stalks, seeds and ribs, and cut into 2 cm dice. Peel and thinly slice the carrot. Peel the pineapple, removing the brown eyes. Quarter lengthwise, discard the core and cut the flesh into 2 cm dice.

3 Heat the oil in a wok or frying pan over medium heat. Add the chicken and stir-fry for 2 to 3 minutes until it lightens in colour. Increase the heat to high and add the sweet peppers, carrot, pineapple, fish sauce, sugar, rice wine and a little water. Stir-fry for about 2 minutes more, or until the vegetables have had time to cook but are still firm and crisp. Transfer to a serving dish and serve immediately.

Variation: This dish tastes good prepared using turkey breast instead of chicken. For special occasions, it is also delicious made with breast of duck.

Chicken with nuts and ginger

Not difficult • Bangkok **Gai pat king** **Serves 4**

5 medium-sized dried wood ear
mushrooms
5 tbsp vegetable oil
100 g unsalted cashew nuts
2 walnut-sized pieces fresh
ginger root
3 spring onions
2 medium-sized tomatoes
3 garlic cloves
400 g boned chicken breasts
2 tbsp fish sauce (nam plah)
2 tbsp oyster sauce
1 tbsp sugar

**Preparation time: 35 minutes
(including soaking time)**

1,700 kJ/400 calories per portion

1 Cover the mushrooms with warm water and leave to soak for about 20 minutes.

2 Meanwhile, heat the oil in a wok or frying pan over medium heat. Stir-fry the cashew nuts for about 3 minutes, until golden. Remove them from the pan with a slotted spoon, drain on kitchen paper and reserve. Leave the oil in the pan, off the heat.

3 Peel and grate the ginger. Trim and wash the spring onions and cut into 3 cm lengths. Wash the tomatoes, remove the stalks and hard core below, and cut into quarters. Drain the mushrooms and squeeze out any excess liquid. Trim any hard parts and cut into quarters.

4 Peel and finely chop the garlic cloves. Rinse the chicken breasts, pat dry and cut into strips about 3 cm long and 1 cm wide.

5 Reheat the oil in the frying pan over medium heat. Fry the garlic for about 2 minutes, until golden. Increase the heat to high, add the chicken strips and fry them for about 2 minutes, until they lighten in colour.

6 Add the ginger, mushrooms, tomatoes, spring onions and cashew nuts, and stir-fry over high heat for about 2 minutes. Reduce the heat and stir in the fish sauce, oyster sauce and sugar. Heat through once more and check for seasoning. If you like, add a little more sugar and fish sauce.

Sweet-and-sour chicken

Gai pat priaw wahn

A little time-consuming • Festive

Serves 4

350 g boned chicken breast
2 tbsp light soy sauce
½ tsp freshly ground black pepper
2 medium-sized tomatoes
2 medium-sized onions
350 g fresh pineapple (peeled weight) or 1 small can pineapple
½ cucumber
1 sweet red pepper
3 garlic cloves
100 g tempura flour
½ litre vegetable oil
2 tsp cornflour
5 tbsp tomato ketchup
3 tbsp fish sauce (nam plah)
12.5 cl pineapple juice (if using fresh pineapple)
3 tbsp rice vinegar or mild wine vinegar
4 tbsp sugar
banana leaves for serving (optional)

Preparation time: 1 hour
(including marinating time)

1,500 kJ/360 calories per portion

1 Wash the chicken, pat dry and cut into 2 cm dice. Season with the soy sauce and black pepper (*above*). Cover and refrigerate for about 30 minutes.

2 Meanwhile, wash the tomatoes, remove the stalks and hard core underneath and cut into quarters. Peel and coarsely dice the onions. Peel the pineapple, remove any brown eyes, quarter lengthwise and remove the core—if using canned pineapple, drain and reserve 12.5 cl of the juice. Chop the pineapple flesh into pieces. Wash the cucumber in hot water and cut into chunks (*above*). Wash and halve the sweet pepper, remove the stalk, ribs and seeds, and dice coarsely. Peel and finely chop the garlic.

3 Preheat the oven to its minimum setting. In a bowl, whisk the tempura flour with a scant ¼ litre water to make a thick, smooth batter, adding a little more water, if necessary. Reserve 3 tbsp of the oil, and heat the rest in a large wok or frying pan. Dip the chicken in the batter to coat, and fry in two or three batches over medium heat for about 4 minutes each batch, until golden. Remove from the oil with a slotted spoon, drain on kitchen paper and place in the oven to keep warm. Discard the cooking oil.

4 In a cup, blend the cornflour with 3 tbsp water until smooth, and leave to stand. Heat the reserved oil in the pan over medium heat. Add the garlic and fry for about 1 minute, until it begins to colour. Increase the heat, add the tomatoes, onions, cucumber, sweet pepper and pineapple, and fry over high heat for 2 minutes more, until the vegetables are crisp but tender (*above*).

5 Add the tomato ketchup and fish sauce to the pan. Reduce the heat, stir in the pineapple juice and return to the boil. Stir in the vinegar and sugar to create a sweet-and-sour flavour—checking and adjusting the flavour as necessary. Stir in the cornflour mixture. Return once more to the boil, stirring frequently, until the sauce thickens.

6 Stir the chicken into the hot sauce, transfer to a serving dish and serve at once. If you like, line the bowl with washed banana leaves.

Chicken in coconut milk

Simple • Fairly hot   Gai gati leuang

Serves 4 to 6

6 chicken thighs
2 tbsp curry powder
5 shallots
½ sweet red pepper
1 can (40 cl) unsweetened coconut milk (see page 135)
2 tsp salt
1 tbsp sugar
2 tbsp lime juice

Preparation time: 55 minutes (including marinating time)

890 kJ/210 calories per portion (if serving 6)

1 Wash the chicken joints, pat dry and rub them all over with the curry powder. Leave to stand for about 20 minutes. Meanwhile, peel and coarsely dice the shallots. Wash the half sweet red pepper, remove the stalk, seeds and ribs and cut into very fine strips about 5 cm long.

2 In a large saucepan, bring the coconut milk to the boil and simmer over medium heat for about 1 minute, stirring constantly. Add the shallots, chicken, salt, sugar and lime juice. Cover, and cook for about 20 minutes. Remove the lid and continue to cook, uncovered, for a further 10 minutes, stirring from time to time, to thicken the sauce. Transfer to a serving dish, garnish with the sweet pepper strips and serve.

Variation: This dish works just as well using other joints of chicken, such as wings or breast, or a combination of breast and thigh joints.

Note: Curry powder, a mixture of a number of tropical spices, was first introduced to Thailand from India. You can make this recipe using either a hot or a milder variety, according to your taste.

Chicken curry

Not difficult • Aromatic   Panaeng gai

Serves 4

500 g boned chicken breast
½ sweet red pepper
2 kaffir lime leaves
50 basil leaves (preferably bai horapah; see page 71)
½ can (20 cl) unsweetened coconut milk (see page 135)
2 tbsp panaeng curry paste (page 26)
2 tbsp fish sauce (nam plah)
3 tbsp sugar

Preparation time: 20 minutes (plus 20 minutes for the curry paste)

1,600 kJ/380 calories per portion

1 Wash the chicken breast, pat dry and cut into bite-sized pieces or thin strips. Wash the half sweet pepper, remove the stalk, ribs and seeds, and cut into very fine strips. Wash the lime leaves, pat dry, roll lengthwise and shred finely. Wash the basil leaves and shake dry.

2 Skim off 1 tbsp of the thick cream from the top of the coconut milk (*see Note, bottom recipe, page 64*) and reserve. In a large saucepan, bring the rest of the milk to the boil. Reduce the heat, stir in the *panaeng* curry paste and simmer gently over low heat for about 1 minute.

3 Add the chicken, fish sauce, sugar and half of the lime leaves to the pan. Cook over low heat for about 5 minutes. Transfer to a serving bowl and stir in the basil leaves. Garnish with the strips of sweet pepper and the remaining lime leaves, and sprinkle with the reserved coconut cream. Serve at once.

Variations: Instead of chicken breast you can use 500 g peeled prawns. Another delicious alternative is thin strips of pork escalope.

Chicken with ginger sauce

Kao man gai

*1 cleaned boiling fowl
(about 1.6 kg)*
8 garlic cloves
5 sprigs fresh coriander with roots
½ tsp freshly ground black pepper
1 tsp salt
*1 walnut-sized piece fresh
ginger root*
*3 fresh bird's-eye chili peppers (see
Glossary)*
*3 tbsp salty brown or black bean
sauce (with whole beans)*
*3 tbsp rice vinegar or mild
wine vinegar*
2 tbsp sweet soy sauce
3 tbsp sugar
1 cucumber
250 g Thai fragrant rice

Preparation time: 2½ hours

2,800 kJ/670 calories per portion

1 Wash the chicken thoroughly inside and out and drain well. Peel the garlic. Wash the coriander and shake dry, tear off the leaves and reserve. Using a pestle and mortar (*above*), or a food processor, crush the coriander roots and stalks, garlic, black pepper and salt to a paste. Rub well over the inside and outside of the chicken.

2 In a large cooking pot, bring about 2.5 litres water to the boil. Carefully place the chicken in the pot, cover and cook gently over medium to low heat for about 2 hours, until tender.

3 Meanwhile, peel the ginger, wash the chili peppers and remove the stalks. Grind the ginger and chilies together with the pestle and mortar, or in a food processor. Strain the bean sauce through a small sieve, reserving the liquid. Add the beans to the mortar or food processor and crush them slightly before stirring into the paste.

4 Mix the ginger paste with the reserved bean liquid, vinegar, soy sauce and sugar. Place in a small

saucepan, briefly boil the sauce, then set aside. Meanwhile, wash the cucumber thoroughly—or, if you prefer, peel it—and cut into 5 mm-thick slices.

5 About 30 minutes before the end of the chicken's cooking time, place the rice in a large pot and add enough of the chicken stock to reach about 2 cm above the surface of the rice. Cover and bring to the boil. Reduce the heat to low and simmer the rice, covered, for about 20 minutes, until the rice has absorbed all the liquid.

6 Remove the chicken from the pan and drain, reserving the stock. Joint the chicken, remove the skin and

bones, and cut the meat into thick slices (*above*). Arrange on a serving dish with the rice, or, if you prefer, serve separately. Garnish with the cucumber slices and the reserved coriander leaves—and, if you like, whole chilies or spring onions. Serve with the lukewarm ginger sauce.

Note: If you like, season the rest of the chicken stock with 2 tbsp fish sauce (*nam plah*) and serve with the chicken. Brown or black bean sauce is sold in "ground" or "whole" form; the latter is needed for this recipe. Fermented black beans are a possible substitute.

Chicken with sweetcorn

Gai pat yort kao poht

Quick and easy • Bangkok

Serves 4 to 6

600 g boned chicken breast
3 tbsp fish sauce (nam plah)
½ tsp freshly ground black pepper
500 g fresh baby sweetcorn
3 spring onions
5 garlic cloves
5 tbsp vegetable oil
2 tbsp oyster sauce
1 tbsp sugar

Preparation time: 25 minutes

870 kJ/210 calories per portion
(if serving 6)

1 Wash the chicken, pat dry and cut into strips about 3 cm long and 5 mm wide. Mix thoroughly with 1 tbsp of the fish sauce and the pepper to coat, and leave to marinate for about 10 minutes.

2 Meanwhile, wash the sweetcorn, trim off the thick ends and halve lengthwise. Wash the spring onions, shake dry, halve lengthwise and cut into pieces about 4 cm long. Peel and finely chop the garlic.

3 Heat the oil in a wok or frying pan over high heat and fry the garlic for about 2 minutes, until golden. Add the chicken strips and toss with the garlic for a further 2 minutes, until the chicken is lightly browned. Add the sweetcorn, spring onions, the remaining fish sauce, the oyster sauce and the sugar, and toss the ingredients together in the pan for about 1 minute more until thoroughly hot. Add a little water if the sauce seems too thick. Transfer to a serving dish and serve immediately.

Variation: This recipe also works well using turkey or pork.

Note: If fresh baby sweetcorn is unavailable, you can use canned. Be sure to buy them canned in water rather than vinegar, and rinse thoroughly before use.

Chicken with sesame seeds

Not difficult • Bangkok   **Gai pat ngah kao**   *Serves 4 to 6*

600 g boned chicken breast
½ tsp freshly ground coriander
seeds
½ tsp salt
2 cm piece fresh ginger root
500 g broccoli stalks
2 tbsp white sesame seeds
3 tbsp vegetable oil
2 tbsp light soy sauce
1 tbsp fish sauce (nam plah)
1 tbsp sugar
1 bowl chilies in vinegar (page 32)

Preparation time: 30 minutes

660 kJ/160 calories per portion
(if serving 6)

1 Wash the chicken, pat dry and cut into strips about 5 cm long and 1 cm wide. Season with the coriander and salt and leave to stand for about 10 minutes.

2 Meanwhile, peel and finely chop the ginger. Peel the broccoli stalks, discarding any woody bits, and cut into thin strips about 5 cm long. Bring a generous litre of water to a brisk boil. Blanch the broccoli in the boiling water for about 1 minute, strain through a colander and leave to drain.

3 In a wok or frying pan, dry-roast the sesame seeds over medium heat for about 2 minutes, until brown, then transfer to a small bowl and set aside. Heat the oil in the pan over high heat, add the chicken and ginger and stir-fry for about 2 minutes, until the chicken is lightly browned.

4 Reduce the heat to medium, add the broccoli, soy sauce, fish sauce, sugar and sesame seeds, and continue to stir-fry for about 2 minutes. Transfer to a serving dish and serve at once, accompanied by the chilies in vinegar.

Note: Try adding a sliced garlic clove to the chilies in vinegar.

Roast duck

Simple, but takes time • Basic recipe

Pet yahng nam peung

Serves 4

1 oven-ready duck (about 2.2 kg)
10 garlic cloves
3 sprigs fresh coriander
½ tsp salt
½ tsp freshly ground black pepper
3 tbsp clear honey
3 tbsp sweet soy sauce
5 tbsp rice vinegar or mild wine vinegar
3 tbsp sugar
1 fresh red jalapeño chili pepper (see Glossary)

Preparation time: 1¾ hours (plus 2 hours' marinating time)

4,300 kJ/1,000 calories per portion

1 Rinse the duck inside and out, and drain. Peel the garlic. Wash the coriander and pat dry. Using a pestle and mortar, or a food processor or blender, crush the garlic and coriander to a paste with the salt and black pepper. Transfer to a small bowl and stir in the honey and 1 tbsp of the soy sauce. Rub the paste over the inside and outside of the duck, cover, and stand in a cool place for about 2 hours to marinate.

2 Meanwhile, in a small saucepan, mix the rice vinegar, the remaining soy sauce and the sugar. Bring briefly to the boil, then allow to cool. Wash the chili, discard the stalk and cut into thin rings. Add to the sauce and set aside.

3 Preheat the oven to 190°C (375°F or Mark 5). Put the duck on a rack in a roasting pan—so that the fat can drip down—and place in the centre of the oven. After 10 minutes, reduce the temperature to 180°C (350°F or Mark 4). Cook for a further 1¼ to 1½ hours, turning and basting with the pan fat from time to time. If the duck browns too fast, cover loosely with aluminium foil. To test for doneness you can push a skewer into the thickest part of the thigh—the juices should run clear. Carve and serve with the vinegar sauce.

Note: This recipe, without the sauce, is the basis of the next two dishes. It is also good just as it is, served with rice and a few cucumber slices.

Red duck curry

Takes time • Festive

Gaeng pet bet yahng

Serves 4 to 6

1 roasted duck (above)
10 cherry tomatoes
5 kaffir lime leaves
20 basil leaves (preferably bai horapah; see page 71)
350 g fresh pineapple (peeled weight) or 1 can pineapple
3 tbsp vegetable oil
2 tbsp red curry paste (page 26)
1 can (40 cl) unsweetened coconut milk (see page 135)
3 tbsp fish sauce (nam plah)
1 tbsp sugar

Preparation time: 30 minutes (plus 4 hours for the duck and curry paste)

3,200 kJ/760 calories per portion (if serving 6)

1 Remove the duck meat from the bones and cut into strips about 4 cm long and 1 cm wide.

2 Wash the tomatoes and lime leaves. Pat the lime leaves dry and cut into quarters. Wash the basil leaves and shake dry. If you are using fresh pineapple, peel, cut out the brown eyes, quarter lengthwise and remove the hard core. If using canned pineapple, drain off the juice. Cut the pineapple flesh into bite-sized pieces.

3 In a wok or large sauté pan, heat the oil over low heat and stir in the curry paste. Skim 5 tbsp cream from the top of the coconut milk (*see Note, bottom*

recipe, page 64) and stir into the pan. Simmer for about 1 minute. Increase the heat to medium, and add the duck, pineapple, lime leaves, sugar fish sauce, and the remaining coconut milk, then cook for another 2 minutes or so, until thoroughly hot.

4 Stir in the tomatoes and basil leaves, transfer to a serving bowl and serve immediately.

Note: For a quicker version of this dish and the next one, you can use only duck breasts, which takes less time to roast than a whole bird.

Duck with tamarind sauce

Takes time • Sweet-and-sour   **Pet makahm**   *Serves 4*

*2 walnut-sized pieces compressed
tamarind pulp*
1 roasted duck (page 111)
15 garlic cloves
8 to 10 shallots
*4 tbsp palm sugar or soft brown
sugar*
3 tbsp fish sauce (nam plah)
8 tbsp vegetable oil

*Preparation time: 30 minutes
(plus 3½ hours for the duck)*

5,000 kJ/1,200 calories per portion

1 Place the tamarind pulp in a small
bowl, cover with lukewarm water
and soak for about 10 minutes. Remove
the duck meat from the bones and cut
into strips about 4 cm long and 1 cm
wide. Peel the garlic and shallots and
slice thinly.

2 Knead the tamarind pulp thoroughly
to produce a thick juice. Discard any
hard bits or seeds, then strain through
a fine sieve into a small saucepan.

3 Add the palm sugar and fish sauce
to the tamarind juice and stir well,
until the sugar has dissolved. Place the
saucepan over medium heat and cook
for about 2 minutes.

4 Heat 5 tbsp of the oil in a wok or
frying pan. Fry the garlic and shallots
together over medium heat for about 3
minutes until golden, then add to the
tamarind sauce, and keep warm.

5 Heat the remaining oil in the pan
over high heat. Add the duck and stir-
fry for about 2 minutes, until heated
through. Drain on kitchen paper and
transfer to a serving dish. Pour the
warm sauce over the duck or, if you
prefer, serve the sauce
separately.

Tamarind

The sour, tangy flavour of tamarind, so characteristic of many Thai dishes, comes from the pods of the tamarind tree, a 20 to 30 metre-high evergreen found all over Asia. The brittle-shelled pods, resembling bean pods in shape, range in colour from greyish brown to cinnamon. The soft, nutty brown pulp they contain—made up of 3 per cent sugar and more than 20 per cent fruit acid—produces the flavouring.

Although fresh tamarinds can sometimes be found in good Oriental food shops, preparing them for cooking is a laborious process. The Thais, however, usually prefer the compressed blocks of tamarind pulp, which are also more easily available here. And there is also ready-prepared tamarind purée, which is sold in jars.

To obtain tamarind juice for seasoning food, soak the compressed pulp in lukewarm water for about 10 minutes, then knead vigorously and squeeze out the dark brown juice. This should be passed through a fine sieve to remove any hard bits and seeds.

In addition to the sour tamarinds used in cooking, there are also sweet varieties, which are usually shelled and eaten raw: tamarind dipped in sugar is a favourite Thai between-meals snack. Boiled in water, sweet tamarinds produce a refreshing drink.

FISH AND SHELLFISH

T hailand is a fish-lover's paradise: the long coastlines of the Gulf of Thailand and the Andaman Sea provide a wealth of saltwater fish and shellfish and there are rich stocks of freshwater fish in the rivers and *klongs*. The rice paddies, too, provide a home for fish. There is a remarkable variety to choose from and shellfish are so plentiful that they are not regarded as a luxury.

Considering the abundance, it is not surprising that for the Thais fish is the most important food after rice. They have turned fish cookery into an art. Fish sauce (*nam plah*) and shrimp paste (*gapi*) are basic flavouring ingredients. Fresh fish is deep or shallow fried, steamed or wrapped in banana leaves and grilled over charcoal. Prawns and squid make delicious stir-fries with vegetables. And both fish and shellfish are used in soups and fiery curries.

The fish you buy should be odourless, firm fleshed and clear eyed; when buying whole fish, get the fishmonger to clean and scale them for you. Live bivalves and other molluscs should be rinsed and, if they are sandy, soaked in cold water before cooking; mussels need debearding. Discard any mussels that do not close when briskly tapped; also discard any that remain closed after being cooked.

Raw lobster should be bought live; crab is sold live or cooked, and also as shelled crab meat or sticks. Prawns are sold fresh or frozen, raw or cooked; squid is available whole or ready cleaned.

Grilled trout

Plah samlee prung rot

Not difficult • Fairly hot

Serves 4

4 cleaned, medium-sized trout, each
weighing 200 to 250 g
12.5 cl lime juice
1 tsp salt
freshly ground black pepper
300 g white cabbage
1 large carrot
10 garlic cloves
12.5 cl vegetable oil
1 tbsp chili powder
2 tbsp sugar
3 tbsp fish sauce (nam plah)
1 banana leaf (optional)

Preparation time: 35 minutes

1,800 kJ/430 calories per portion

1 Wash the trout in cold water and pat dry. Make shallow incisions at 2 cm intervals along both sides of each fish. In a small bowl mix 4 tbsp of the lime juice with the salt and brush over the fish, inside and out. Sprinkle with a little freshly ground black pepper.

2 Trim and wash the cabbage and carrot, and shred very finely. Peel and finely chop the garlic.

3 Heat 5 tbsp of the oil in a small saucepan over medium heat. Fry the garlic for about 2 minutes, until golden. Transfer the garlic and oil to a small bowl. Preheat the grill to a fairly high heat or light a charcoal grill.

4 In the same pan, heat another 2 tbsp of the oil and briefly fry the chili powder. Remove from the heat. Add the sugar, fish sauce and remaining lime juice, and stir until the sugar dissolves.

5 Brush the trout with the remaining oil and grill for 5 to 7 minutes each side, brushing with a little extra oil during cooking.

6 Meanwhile, line a serving dish or four plates with pieces of the banana leaf, if using. Arrange the shredded vegetables round the edges. Place the fish in the centre and sprinkle with the garlic and the lukewarm chili sauce, or serve the sauce separately.

Sole with lime sauce

Not difficult • Central Thailand

Plah neung manao

Serves 4

8 sole fillets, or 2 whole sole filleted
10 garlic cloves
5 or 9 fresh red bird's-eye chili
peppers (see Glossary)
30 g chives
5 tbsp lime juice
1 tsp salt
3 tbsp light soy sauce

Preparation time: 40 minutes

700 kJ/170 calories per portion

1 Rinse the fillets briefly under cold running water, pat dry and place the fish in an ovenproof baking dish. Preheat the oven to 200°C (400°F or Mark 6).

2 Peel and thinly slice the garlic. Wash the chili peppers, remove the stalks, and cut 5 chilies into thin rings. Wash the chives, shake dry and cut them into 3 cm lengths.

3 In a small bowl, mix the cut chili peppers, garlic, lime juice, salt and soy sauce with about 12.5 cl water, until thoroughly blended. Pour over the fish and bake in the centre of the

oven for about 20 minutes. Transfer to 4 individual plates or a serving dish, sprinkle with the chopped chives and serve, garnished, if you like, with whole fresh chili peppers cut into flowers (*see step 4, page 92*).

Variation: In Thailand this dish is often made with a whole fish, such as butterfish. To prepare a whole fish, rinse and pat dry and make shallow incisions at 2 cm intervals along each side. Dentex, bass or halibut are also suitable for this recipe.

Note: If you have a steamer, you can steam the fish for 25 minutes, rather than baking it.

Crawfish with tamarind

More complex • Festive

Gung yahng raht sot

*4 medium-sized live crawfish, or
spiny lobsters, each weighing
about 900 g
15 cl vegetable oil
freshly ground black pepper
2 walnut-sized pieces compressed
tamarind pulp
10 garlic cloves
7 shallots
3 sprigs fresh coriander with roots
2 fresh red bird's-eye chili peppers
(see Glossary)
4 tbsp palm sugar or soft brown
sugar
3 tbsp fish sauce (nam plah)
lettuce leaves for garnish*

Preparation time: 1 hour

2,300 kJ/550 calories per portion

1 Preheat the oven to 180°C (350°F or Mark 4). Bring a large pan of salted water to the boil and, grasping each one by the back, drop the crawfish into the boiling water. Cook for 2 minutes then remove and cool. With a heavy knife or cleaver cut off the heads and reserve. With the knife, split through the underside of each body shell from head to tail and prise open with your hands to reveal the meat beneath. Leaving the tail attached to the body, remove the gravel-sac (or stomach), the vein-like intestinal canal (*above*) and any loose bits of shell, and discard. Wash the crawfish and pat dry.

2 Line a baking sheet with aluminium foil and brush with 1 tbsp oil. Arrange the crawfish on the foil, sprinkle with a little pepper, and brush each with 1 tbsp oil. Bake in the centre of the oven for about 20 minutes, basting from time to time with the cooking juices.

3 Meanwhile, soak the tamarind pulp in 12.5 cl warm water for about 10 minutes. Peel and slice the garlic and shallots. Wash the coriander, shake dry and tear off the leaves. Using a pestle and mortar, crush the coriander stalks and roots with a little pepper. Wash and halve the chilies, remove the stalks and seeds, and chop finely—if you like, cut half a chili into thin rings.

4 Knead the soaked tamarind pulp thoroughly, to produce a thick, dark juice (*above*). Discard any hard bits or seeds, then strain through a fine sieve into a bowl.

5 Heat 5 tbsp of the oil in a frying pan over medium heat and fry the garlic and shallots for about 2 minutes, until golden. Reserve, including the oil.

6 Add the sugar, fish sauce and chopped chili peppers to the tamarind juice and stir until the sugar has dissolved. Heat the remaining oil in a small saucepan, add the crushed coriander stalks and roots, and fry briefly over a low heat. Stir in the tamarind and chili sauce and simmer for about 1 minute more. Mix with the reserved garlic, shallots and oil.

7 Line a warmed serving dish with lettuce leaves and arrange the crawfish on top together with the reserved heads. Pour over the sauce and garnish with coriander leaves. Serve at once.

Note: Crawfish, or spiny lobster, has drier meat than lobster, and must be moistened frequently while cooking. If crawfish are unavailable, lobsters can be substituted.

Grilled fish parcels

Ngop plah

Needs a little care • Special occasions

400 g redfish or cod fillets
4 tbsp fish sauce (nam plah)
½ tsp freshly ground black pepper
10 kaffir lime leaves
100 g minced pork
100 g minced beef
2 tbsp red curry paste (page 26)
7 tbsp thick coconut milk or coconut cream (see page 135)
2 eggs
2 large banana leaves

*Preparation time: 1 hour
(plus 25 minutes for the curry paste)*

1,200 kJ/290 calories per portion

1 Rinse the fish under running water, pat dry, and cut crosswise into 1 cm-wide strips. Mix with 1 tbsp of the fish sauce and the black pepper to season. Cover and place in the refrigerator for about 10 minutes to marinate.

2 Meanwhile, wash the lime leaves and pat dry. Roll lengthwise, and shred finely. In a large bowl, mix the minced pork and beef with the curry paste and the coconut milk or cream. Add the rest of the fish sauce and the lime leaves, break the eggs into the bowl and blend thoroughly. Carefully stir in the fish.

3 Wipe the banana leaves clean with a damp cloth and cut each one crosswise into four strips, about 20 cm wide. Place the strips in pairs, one on top of the other, to make four double-thickness wrappers. Divide the fish mixture equally into four and place in the middle of each leaf (*above*).

4 Preheat a grill to a fairly high heat or light a charcoal grill until it glows. Meanwhile, fold the banana leaves into roughly rectangular packages by bringing the long edges together over the fish so that they meet in the middle and overlap by 2 to 3 cm. If necessary, secure with toothpicks. Then fold in the ends to meet in the middle, and secure with toothpicks (*above*).

5 If using a charcoal grill, grill the stuffed banana leaves for about 15 minutes, turning from time to time. It does not matter if the outer leaves turn completely black. If you are using a conventional grill, cook for about 20 minutes, turning from time to time. Transfer to a serving dish and serve, leaving each diner to open his or her own parcel at the table.

Note: Banana leaves, which are not edible, are available from Asian food stores. If you cannot find them, you can wrap the fish mixture in a double layer of aluminium foil instead. This will not, however, give the dish its authentic flavour and aroma. If using canned coconut milk, use the cream off the top (*see Note, bottom recipe, page 64*).

Fish and Shellfish 121

Baked fish in banana leaves
Hor mok plah

Serves 4

200 g white cabbage
5 kaffir lime leaves
½ sweet red pepper
500 g redfish, cod or pollack fillets
4 garlic cloves
½ tsp freshly ground black pepper
3 tbsp red curry paste (page 26)
1 can (40 cl) unsweetened coconut milk (see page 135)
1 egg
4 tbsp fish sauce (nam plah)
2 large banana leaves
½ tsp cornflour

Preparation time: 1½ hours
(plus 25 minutes for the curry paste)

850 kJ/200 calories per portion

1 Bring a saucepan of water to the boil. Meanwhile, trim the cabbage, remove the hard core, shred finely and wash. Blanch in the briskly boiling water for about 1 minute, then drain well in a colander.

2 Wash the lime leaves, pat dry, roll up lengthwise and shred very finely. Wash the sweet pepper half, remove the stalk, ribs and seeds, and slice thinly. Rinse the fish under cold running water and pat dry. Reserve about a fifth of the fish, and cut the rest into very thin strips about 4 cm long.

3 Peel the garlic. Using a pestle and mortar or a food processor or blender, grind the garlic, the reserved fish and the black pepper to a creamy paste. Stir in the red curry paste, and transfer the mixture to a large bowl. Skim off about 4 tbsp cream from the top of the coconut milk (*see Note, bottom recipe, page 64*) and reserve. Add the rest to the paste. Using an egg whisk (or a hand-held electric whisk on a low setting), beat the paste for about 3 minutes until smooth.

4 Preheat the oven to 180°C (350°F or Mark 4). Break the egg into the paste and add the fish sauce and most of the chopped lime leaves. Whisk for about 1 minute more before carefully stirring in the sliced fish.

5 Wipe the banana leaves clean with a damp cloth and lay on a chopping board. Using a bowl about 15 cm in diameter as a guide and a sharp knife, cut out six circles from each leaf.

6 In each circle, make four evenly-spaced 5 cm-long incisions from the edge towards the middle (*above*).

7 Shape the leaf circles into small bowls, making sure that they overlap along the incisions to seal. Secure each overlap with toothpicks (*above*).

8 Line each leaf bowl with some shredded cabbage and fill with the fish mixture. Arrange in a roasting pan, or baking tray, and bake in the centre of the oven for about 20 minutes.

9 Meanwhile, mix the reserved coconut cream with the cornflour and 4 tbsp water and stir until smooth. Transfer to a small pan, bring to the boil, stirring constantly until the sauce thickens. To serve, pour a little of the sauce over each leaf bowl. Garnish with the remaining lime leaves and the sweet pepper, and serve immediately.

Prawns with asparagus

Not difficult • Bangkok

Gung pat nor mai farang

Serves 4

600 g medium-sized raw prawns
4 tbsp fish sauce (nam plah)
½ tsp freshly ground black pepper
500 g green asparagus
5 garlic cloves
5 tbsp vegetable oil
3 tbsp oyster sauce
1 tbsp sugar
2 tbsp rice wine (or, if unavailable, medium-dry sherry)

Preparation time: 30 minutes

1,200 kJ/290 calories per portion

1 Wash and shell the prawns, leaving the tails on and removing the dark, vein-like intestines. Mix the prawns with 1 tbsp of the fish sauce and the ground black pepper, and set aside.

2 Bring a generous amount of water to the boil in a large saucepan. Snap the woody bottoms from the asparagus, and peel each spear and wash. Cut the spears into 4 cm-long pieces and blanch for about 1 minute in the boiling water. Drain well in a colander. Peel and finely chop the garlic.

3 Heat the oil in a wok or frying pan and fry the garlic for about 1 minute. Add the prawns and fry over high heat

for a further minute. Add the asparagus, the oyster sauce, the remaining fish sauce, the sugar and the rice wine, and stir-fry for about 2 minutes more. If the pan juices become too thick, add a little water. Transfer to a serving dish and serve at once.

Note: Asparagus must be completely fresh and crisp and should be prepared just before cooking. When buying, especially if pre-packed, check spear ends for signs of dryness; if they are moist, the asparagus is fresh. Young, tender spears are best for this recipe: more mature asparagus may need 5 or more minutes cooking in Step 2.

Clams with basil

Not difficult • Special occasions

Hoy lai pat

Serves 4 to 6

2 kg live clams, cockles or Venus
mussels
10 garlic cloves
30 fresh basil leaves (preferably bai
horapah; see page 71)
50 g butter
½ tsp salt
1 banana leaf (optional)
1 sprig basil, for garnish

Preparation time: 30 minutes
(plus 2 hours' soaking time)

600 kJ/140 calories per portion
(if serving 6)

1 Tap sharply any shells that are open and discard those that don't close. Soak the rest in cold, salted water for about 2 hours, changing the water if it becomes muddy, then scrub thoroughly with a stiff brush. Bring ¼ litre water to the boil in a large pan, add the shellfish, cover the pan and cook over high heat until the shells open. Discard any that remain closed. Remove and discard the empty half shells.

2 Peel and finely chop the garlic. Wash the basil leaves, shake dry, and reserve. In a large wok or frying pan, heat the butter over medium heat. Add the garlic and fry for about 2 minutes,

until golden. Increase the heat to high, add the shellfish, salt and basil leaves and stir-fry for about 3 minutes.

3 Transfer the shellfish to a large serving dish, lined, if you like, with a washed banana leaf. Pour over the pan juices and garnish with the sprig of basil. Serve immediately.

Note: In Thailand, where butter is not so widely available, oil is the common frying medium. For the subtle flavours of this dish, however, butter is preferred. Thais prefer bivalves undercooked—and also eat them raw, sprinkled with lime juice—so the precooking in Step 1 is usually omitted and the live shellfish are prised open with a sharp knife.

Fried crab with celery

Quick and easy • Most occasions

Poo pat pong garee

Serves 4 to 6

**800 g frozen crab meat sticks,
thawed**
400 g celery
8 garlic cloves
5 tbsp oil
1 tsp curry powder
3 tbsp fish sauce (nam plah)
1 tbsp sugar

Preparation time: 25 minutes

*870 kJ/210 calories per portion
(if serving 6)*

1 Wash the crab sticks, pat dry and cut into pieces 4 cm long. Wash the celery and shake dry. Separate into sticks, trim the woody ends and halve the thicker sticks lengthwise. Cut into 4 cm pieces.

2 Peel and finely chop the garlic. Heat the oil in a wok or frying pan and fry the garlic over medium heat for about 2 minutes, until golden. Increase the heat to high, add the crab and fry for about 1 minute, then add the curry powder and stir well. Add the chopped celery, the fish sauce, the sugar and a little water, and continue to cook for a further 2 minutes. Transfer to a warm serving dish and serve immediately.

Note: Frozen crab sticks are available from larger supermarkets, some fishmongers and Asian food stores. They are a convenient alternative to whole crab. In Thailand, where whole crabs are widely available, this dish is made with live crabs; everything except the main shell is fried and served with the other ingredients and diners suck the meat out of the claws and legs.

Garlic prawns

Fairly easy • Festive

Gung gratiam prik thai

Serves 4

**12 raw deep sea prawns in their
shells, thawed if frozen**
10 garlic cloves
2 tbsp fish sauce (nam plah)
½ tsp freshly ground black pepper
2 tbsp lime juice
3 medium-sized tomatoes
¼ cucumber
30 g chives
50 g butter

Preparation time: 30 minutes

880 kJ/210 calories per portion

1 Wash and shell the prawns, leaving the tails on and removing the dark, vein-like intestines. Rinse under cold water and pat dry with kitchen paper.

2 Peel and finely chop the garlic. In a bowl, mix the prawns, chopped garlic, fish sauce, black pepper and the lime juice. Leave to marinate for about 10 minutes.

3 Meanwhile, wash and halve the tomatoes and the cucumber and cut them into 5 mm thick slices. Wash the chives, shake dry and cut into small pieces. Arrange the tomatoes and cucumber slices round the edge of a serving dish.

4 In a wok or large frying pan, melt the butter over medium heat. Remove the prawns from the marinade with a slotted spoon and add to the pan. Stir a little water into the marinade and add to the prawns. Cook, uncovered, over medium heat for about 5 minutes.

5 Transfer the prawns and pan juices to the serving dish and sprinkle with the chives. Serve at once.

Variation: This recipe also works well with squid. Wash about 600 g cleaned squid pouches and cut them into 1 cm-thick rings. Cook in the same way as the prawns.

DESSERTS

T hai desserts in all their tropical variety are eaten, as in Europe, to round off a meal—and to cool burning tastebuds. Most are based on Thailand's wonderful fruits.

The simplest dessert is a bowl of fresh fruits, which in Thailand, like raw vegetables, are often carved into appealing shapes (*see page 97*). Depending on the season, a fruit bowl may include papayas, mangoes, melons, oranges, rambutans, lychees or the smaller, similar-tasting, longans—also known as "dragon's eyes".

Fruits such as pineapples and bananas are fried in tempura batter to make delicious fritters—also popular as between-meals snacks. And mangoes, with their fragrance and delicate sweet-and-sour flavour, lend themselves to a range of presentations. In Thailand, there are more than a dozen varieties of mangoes, available between March and June. The flesh melds especially well with glutinous rice and coconut milk (*page 132*) .

Coconut milk, an essential ingredient of both savoury and sweet dishes in southern Thailand where coconuts are grown on plantations, is used in many ways in desserts; as well as in glutinous rice dishes and served with fruit, it is a favourite flavouring in ice cream and puddings such as the coconut custards on page 134.

Oranges in liqueur

Som loy gao

Simple • Prepare in advance

Serves 4

4 large oranges
100 g brown sugar
12.5 cl orange-flavoured liqueur
(such as Cointreau)

Preparation time: 35 minutes
(plus 12 hours' macerating time)

980 kJ/230 calories per portion

1 Peel the oranges with a sharp knife, making sure to remove all the pith. Cut the flesh into slices about 1 cm thick, removing any pips.

2 Place the sugar with about ½ litre water in a small saucepan, and cook over medium heat for about 20 minutes, stirring occasionally, until a thick syrup forms. Remove from the heat and leave to cool.

3 In a bowl, gently but thoroughly mix the syrup, the oranges and the liqueur. Place in the refrigerator and leave for at least 12 hours, or overnight.

4 To serve, re-form the orange slices into four oranges and secure with cocktail sticks. Place on a dish and pour over the syrup. For a more alcoholic dessert, pour over a little additional liqueur just before serving.

Variations: Serve the slices flambéed by heating a high-alcohol orange liqueur in a spoon, igniting and pouring over the oranges. Alternatively, serve with orange ice cream.

Note: A few washed, fresh mint leaves make an attractive garnish and go well with the orange flavour.

Melon with coconut milk

Taeng thai nam gati

Not difficult • Prepare in advance

Serves 4

1 honeydew or cantaloupe melon
1 can (40 cl) unsweetened
coconut milk (see page 135)
5 tbsp palm sugar or soft
brown sugar
½ vanilla pod
mint leaves (optional)

Preparation time: 20 minutes
(plus 1 hour's chilling time)

560 kJ/130 calories per portion

1 Peel the melon, cut lengthwise into quarters, and scoop out the seeds with a spoon. Cut the flesh into bite-sized pieces, cover and leave in the refrigerator for about 1 hour.

2 Meanwhile, put the coconut milk and palm sugar in a small saucepan. Cut the vanilla pod half open lengthwise and, with the point of a knife, scrape the seeds into the pan. Heat gently over low heat, stirring constantly, until all the sugar has dissolved. Allow to cool briefly, then place in the refrigerator.

3 Transfer the chilled melon to a serving bowl and pour over the vanilla-flavoured coconut milk. If you like, garnish with a few washed mint leaves.

Variation: Mix a can of sweetcorn (about 340 g), thoroughly washed and drained, with the melon.

Note: An alternative way of preparing this dessert is to cut the melon in half lengthwise and, using a melon-baller, scoop out the flesh. To serve, place the halved melon shells on a bed of crushed ice in a serving bowl, fill the shells with the melon balls and pour over the vanilla-flavoured coconut milk.

Water melon, which has a watery consistency and a weak flavour, is not suitable for this dish.

Mango with glutinous rice

Kao niaw moon mamuang *Serves 4*

100 g glutinous round-grain rice
½ can (20 cl) unsweetened
coconut milk (see page 135)
½ tsp cornflour
salt
3 tbsp sugar
2 ripe mangoes

Preparation time 40 minutes
(plus 12 hours' soaking time)

820 kJ/200 calories per portion

1 Soak the rice for about 12 hours or overnight in cold water. Rinse and drain thoroughly through a fine sieve.

2 Place the rice in a saucepan with water to a level about 1 cm above the rice. Bring to the boil over high heat, reduce the heat to low and cook, covered, for about 20 minutes, until the rice has absorbed all the water. Remove the lid and leave to cool.

3 Skim 2 tbsp of cream from the top of the coconut milk (*see Note, bottom recipe, page 64*) and place in a small saucepan. Add the cornflour, a little salt and about 10 cl water. Stir until smooth, bring briefly to the boil over medium heat, and set aside.

4 Place the rest of the coconut milk in a large saucepan. Stir in the sugar and about 12.5 cl water, and bring briefly to the boil over medium heat. Remove from the heat and stir in the rice.

5 Peel the mangoes with a sharp knife. Halve, deseed and cut into slices.

6 Divide the rice between four individual dishes and arrange half a sliced mango on each. To serve, pour the coconut sauce over the rice.

Note: Both Asian and South American mangoes are suitable for this dish. Asian mangoes, however, have a more delicious flavour.

Tapioca flour rolls in syrup

Kanom luamit *Serves 4 to 6*

300 g tapioca flour
3 different food colourings—for
example, green, red and yellow
500 g sugar
1 vanilla pod

Preparation time: 1½ hours
(plus 15 minutes' cooling time)

1,900 kJ/450 calories per portion
(if serving 6)

1 Bring about 1.25 litres water to the boil in a large pan. Divide the flour equally between three bowls. In a cup or small bowl, mix 2 tbsp flour from the first bowl with 2 tbsp of boiling water. Stir in a few drops of a food colouring. Gradually add another 6 tbsp water and stir until smooth. Mix with the remaining flour in the bowl and knead to a smooth dough. Repeat with the other two bowls of flour, using a different colouring each time.

2 With your hands, shape the dough into 5 to 6 cm rolls—about 1 tsp dough per roll. Prepare three small bowls of cold water. Cook the rolls in separate-

coloured batches in the pan of boiling water over medium heat. They are cooked when they rise to the surface. With a slotted spoon, transfer them from the pan directly to a bowl of cold water, one colour to each bowl.

3 In a small pan, simmer 40 cl water with the sugar for about 20 minutes, stirring until the sugar dissolves. Halve the vanilla pod lengthwise and, with the tip of a knife, scrape the seeds into the syrup. Leave to cool for 15 minutes.

4 Drain the rolls and place in serving bowls according to colour. Pour over the sugar syrup and serve.

Coconut custards

Sangkayah nah gati

Takes time • Southern Thailand

Serves 4 to 5

10 eggs
1½ cans (about 60 cl) unsweetened
coconut milk (see Box, opposite)
500 g palm sugar or soft
brown sugar
2 tbsp rice flour
¼ tsp salt

Preparation time: 1¼ hours
(plus 1 hour's cooling time)

2,100 kJ/500 calories per portion
(if serving 5)

1 Preheat the oven to 150°C (300°F or Mark 2). Break the eggs into a mixing bowl and whisk until blended. In another bowl, mix 40 cl of the coconut milk with the sugar until smooth and creamy. Carefully and slowly stir in the beaten eggs, skimming any froth from the surface with a spoon (otherwise there will be holes in the custard) and transfer the mixture to individual heatproof moulds or ramekins.

2 Stand the moulds or ramekins in a roasting pan or baking dish. Carefully fill the pan with warm water to 1 to 2 cm below the top of the moulds. Place in the centre of the oven and bake for about 50 minutes, until the custards are set. Remove from the oven and leave to cool.

3 Meanwhile, put the remaining coconut milk in a small pan, add the rice flour and salt, and stir together until smooth. Bring the mixture to the boil over medium heat, stirring constantly, and continue to cook for about 2 minutes, until it thickens to a creamy consistency. Leave to cool, then place in a piping bag with a large star-shaped nozzle, and decorate each coconut custard. Either serve lukewarm at once or place in the refrigerator and serve well chilled.

Note: The water in the roasting pan should not be allowed to boil, otherwise there will be holes in the custard, which should be smooth and firm.

Coconut

Coconuts grow on vast plantations in southern Thailand. Their white flesh, grated and soaked, produces coconut milk. This milk has an importance in Thai cuisine similar to that of cow's milk here, and shares many of its properties. Unlike the juice found inside the nut, generally only drunk as a refreshing beverage, coconut milk is fundamental to many dishes—including soups, curries, stews and desserts.

To make fresh coconut milk is a laborious process: the flesh has to be grated, covered with boiling water, then allowed to cool before being squeezed through fine muslin.

It is far simpler to buy unsweetened coconut milk in cans, or in compressed blocks of creamed coconut that can be reconstituted with water. Sweetened milk is also sold, but is useful for only a few desserts.

Where a recipe calls for coconut cream, refrigerate the milk: the cream will rise to the top and can be skimmed off with a spoon.

Banana fritters

Kluay tort

Not difficult • Festive

Serves 4

2 large bananas
50 g tempura flour
1 tbsp sugar
salt
3 tbsp coconut flakes (or, if unavailable, shredded coconut)
1 tbsp light sesame seeds
1 litre vegetable oil
4 tbsp clear honey

Preparation time: 20 minutes

2,100 kJ/500 calories per portion

1 Peel the bananas, halve lengthwise, and cut each half crosswise into two equal pieces.

2 In a shallow bowl, mix the flour with a scant 12.5 cl water, the sugar and a little salt. Stir the mixture until it becomes a smooth, thick batter. Add the coconut flakes and sesame seeds and stir thoroughly.

3 Heat the oil in a large pan until small bubbles rise from a wooden spoon handle dipped into the oil. Dip the banana pieces in the batter to coat them, and deep fry in batches over high heat for about 2 minutes, until the batter is crisp and golden-brown. Remove from the oil with a slotted spoon, drain thoroughly, and place on kitchen paper to absorb any excess oil.

4 Arrange on a serving dish, pour over the honey and serve.

Note: Tempura flour is essential for making the batter. No other flour, such as wheat or rice flour, gives this dessert the same authentic flavour.

Glutinous rice with longans

Kao niaw piak lamyai

Not difficult • Northern Thailand

Serves 4

160 g glutinous short-grain rice
1 can longans
250 g sugar
1 small can (about 16 cl) unsweetened coconut milk (see page 135)
½ tsp salt

Preparation time: 50 minutes (plus 40 minutes' soaking time)

1,900 kJ/450 calories per portion

1 Soak the rice in lukewarm water for about 40 minutes, then drain well through a sieve. Drain the longans, reserving the juice. Pour the juice into a measuring jug and add water to make 70 cl of liquid.

2 Put the rice and the diluted longan juice in a saucepan and bring to the boil, then cook, uncovered, over medium heat for about 30 minutes, until the mixture thickens.

3 Stir the longan fruit and the sugar into the rice, then transfer to a serving bowl.

4 Pour the coconut milk into a small saucepan, add the salt and bring to the boil, stirring constantly. Pour over the warm rice and serve at once.

Variation: Instead of longans, you can use the same quantity of rinsed, canned sweetcorn, but in this case use 70 cl water only to boil the rice.

Note: Fresh longans are sometimes available from Asian or Oriental food stores between July and September, when they are harvested in Thailand. If using fresh longans for this recipe, peel and stone them, and replace the canned juice with water.

Suggested Menus

At a meal in Thailand there are no set courses. With the exception of desserts, which are usually served at the end, the Thais like eating many different kinds of dishes at the same time, and with as many friends and relations as possible to share them. Nobody wants to be thought stingy—a major disgrace in Thailand—so it is preferable to serve too much rather than too little. The suggestions below for combining recipes allow both for very simple meals of only two or three dishes and for more elaborate menus for parties or entertaining dinner guests. Once you are familiar with some of the recipes, you can be more adventurous: try out your own combinations and variations. Discover the broad spectrum of flavours offered by Thai cuisine.

I *Sections marked with a star indicate that Thai fragrant rice (page 82) should be served with each menu.*

Simple or lunch menus

Chicken soup with lemon grass	52
Fried rice with seafood	80
Banana fritters	136
Stuffed cucumber soup	61
Curried chicken rice	82
Papaya salad	92
Fish soup with coconut milk	57
Chicken with nuts and ginger	101
Fried rice with prawns	78
Spring rolls	40
Curried chicken rice	82
Pork fillet with pineapple	74
Beef with green peppercorns	66
Stuffed glutinous rice balls	51
Beef with oyster sauce	64
Prawns with asparagus	124
Chicken curry	105
Thai fragrant rice	82
Spring rolls	40
Fried rice with seafood	80
Fresh fruit	—
Vegetable platter with dip	96
Chicken with ginger sauce	106
Melon with coconut milk	130
Meat and prawn parcels	45
Rice noodles with squid	84
Pork satay	73
Egg noodles with bean sprouts	85

Meatballs with pineapple	42
Stir-fried noodles	87
Fried prawns	50
Noodle soup with red meat	54
Fresh fruit	—
Meat and prawn parcels	45
Fried rice with prawns	78
Melon with coconut milk	130

☆ Menus you can prepare in advance

Three-friends curry	78
Chicken with sesame seeds	109
Roast duck	111
Green beef curry	70
Prawns with asparagus	124
Piquant chicken salad	90
Sweet-and-sour meatballs	75
Oranges in liqueur	130
Chicken curry	105
Pork fillet with pineapple	74
Chicken with ginger sauce	106
Stir-fried vegetables	94
Coconut custards	134

☆ Menus for 6 to 8 people

Green beef curry	70
Chicken with sesame seeds	109
Fried prawns	50
Clams with basil	125
Pork fillet with pineapple	74
Beef with oyster sauce	64
Chicken curry	105
Chili prawns	46
Fish soup with coconut milk	57
Sweet-and-sour meatballs	75
Beef with green beans	67
Glutinous rice with longans	136
Red duck curry	111
Sweet-and-sour meatballs	75
Stir-fried vegetables	94
Fresh fruit	—
Hot prawn dip	37
Vegetable platter with dip	96
Garlic prawns	126
Stuffed cucumber soup	61
Banana fritters	136

☆ Family menus

Yellow beef curry	68
Sole with lime sauce	117
Grilled fish parcels	121
Fresh fruit	—
Chicken soup with lemon grass	52
Shrimp paste dip	35
Vegetable platter with dip	96
Chicken curry	105
Fried crab with celery	126
Sweet-and-sour chicken	102
Melon with coconut milk	130
Three-friends curry	78
Chicken with pineapple	100
Chicken with ginger sauce	106
Stir-fried vegetables	94
Coconut custards	134

☆ Party menus for 10 to 15 people

Piquant chicken salad	90
Beef soup with chilies	58
Prawns with asparagus	124
Fried crab with celery	126
Mango with glutinous rice	132
Chicken soup with lemon grass	52
Sweet-and-sour meatballs	75
Beef with green beans	67
Garlic prawns	126
Beef curry	64
Sweet-and-sour chicken	102
Pork fillet with pineapple	74
Stir-fried vegetables	94
Oranges in liqueur	130
Beef salad with coriander	89
Stir-fried vegetables	94
Chicken with pineapple	100
Yellow beef curry	68
Minced beef salad	88
Fish soup with coconut milk	57
Chicken in coconut milk	105
Chicken with pineapple	100
Fresh fruit	—
Fried prawns	50
Beef with green peppercorns	66
Chicken with sweetcorn	108
Pork fillet with pineapple	74

Chicken soup with lemon grass	52
Beef with oyster sauce	64
Beef with green beans	67
Grilled trout	116
Melon with coconut milk	130

☆ Party menus for special occasions (for 15)

Fried prawns	50
Pork with bamboo shoots	76
Chicken with pineapple	100
Grilled fish parcels	121
Stir-fried vegetables	94
Banana fritters	136
Garlic prawns	126
Beef curry	64
Grilled trout	116
Stir-fried vegetables	94
Glutinous rice with longans	136
Green beef curry	70
Duck with tamarind sauce	112
Grilled fish parcels	121
Oranges in liqueur	130
Meat and prawn parcels	45
Fiery prawn soup	56
Beef curry	64
Chicken with nuts and ginger	101
Pork fillet with pineapple	74
Oranges in liqueur	130

☆ Thai buffet

A buffet consisting of both hot and cold dishes

Spring rolls	40
Meat and prawn parcels	45
Chili prawns	46
Piquant chicken salad	90
Beef salad with coriander	89
Squid salad	90
Fish soup with coconut milk	57
Beef soup with chilies	58
Chicken soup with lemon grass	52
Beef with oyster sauce	64
Green beef curry	70
Chicken curry	105
Roast duck	111
Chicken with pineapple	100
Prawns with asparagus	124
Oranges in liqueur	130
Melon with coconut milk	130
Tapioca flour rolls in syrup	132
Banana fritters	136

Glossary

This Glossary is intended as a brief guide to some less familiar cookery terms and ingredients, including words or items found on Thai menus.

Aubergine: a vegetable fruit with a mildly sweet flavour, most commonly available in Europe in its purple, elongated form. Many different varieties of aubergine are used in Thai cuisine: from tiny pea aubergines, which are added to dishes shortly before the end of cooking, to white, yellow or green ones—about the size of small tomatoes—which are halved or quartered before cooking. Where these are unavailable, substitute the purple variety cut into comparably sized pieces.

Bamboo shoots: edible young shoots of the bamboo plant. *See also page 77.*

Banana flowers: the flowers of the banana tree, whose tender, edible hearts can be eaten raw, in salads or added to stir-fried dishes.

Banana leaves: the glossy, dark green leaves of the banana tree, used to line steamers or to wrap foods, such as chicken or fish, prior to grilling or baking.

Basil: a pungent herb, much used in Mediterranean regions and in Southeast Asia. Three varieties of basil are used in Thai cuisine. S*ee also page 71.*

Bean sprouts: the young sprouts of mung or other beans, used in salads and stir-fried dishes. Rich in vitamins, protein and iron, they are readily available fresh from supermarkets and Asian food shops, or can be grown at home from untreated bean seeds.

Blanch: to plunge food into boiling water for a short time; it helps to remove strong flavours and softens vegetables before furthur cooking. The best way to blanch vegetables is to lower them in a metal collander into boiling water.

Bean sauces and pastes: flavouring agents in Oriental cuisines. Made from fermented yellow, red or black soy beans, there are many varieties, both puréed and containing whole beans, some very salty,

some mild or sweet; hot bean sauce has added chilies. The brown, or black, bean sauce in Thai recipes has a strong, salty flavour and is often used in place of salt.

Cashew nuts: the sweet, kidney-shaped nuts of the cashew tree which flourishes in many parts of Southeast Asia. Usually sold shelled, they are delicious eaten raw or added to salads and stir-fried dishes. Use unsalted nuts for cooking.

Cellophane noodles (also called bean thread noodles): transparent noodles made from mung beans or other vegetable starch. Available in varying round or flat thicknesses, they become soft and slippery when soaked in hot water.

Chili peppers: hot red or green peppers of the capsicum family, ranging from the very hot Thai bird's-eye chili to milder varieties such as the jalapeño. Chilies contain volatile oils that can irritate the skin and cause eyes to burn, so handle them with caution and always wash your hands immediately after using them. The seeds of the chili are its hottest part; this should be taken into account when using either fresh or dried chili peppers. *See also page 31.*

Chili powder: powder made from dried, ground chili peppers. Fresh chili powder is very hot; when stored for any length of time, however, it loses its fieriness and bright red colour. It is readily available.

Chili sauce: hot red or orange sauce made from chili peppers, vinegar and salt. It comes in various strengths and is used in cooking and as a condiment.

Chinese cabbage (also called Chinese leaves): an elongated cabbage, used in soups and cooked dishes or in salads.

Chinese keys (*krachai*): a strange-looking root of the ginger family, most commonly found in Thai and Indonesian cuisine, where it is added to curries and pickles. The fleshy, stronger-flavoured head from which the roots grow is also used in some Southeast Asian cuisine.

Chinese long beans: thin green beans, resembling French beans, that can grow

up to 90 cm long. Usually sold in bunches, they can be found in Asian food stores.

Coconut milk: liquid made from grated coconut flesh and water—not the fresh liquid found inside the coconut. An essential ingredient of many Thai dishes, it is available in cans or compressed blocks. *See also page 135.*

Coriander: the leaves and seeds of the coriander plant, both common seasonings in Mediterranean, Indian and Southeast Asian cooking. *See also page 47.*

Cornflour: very fine flour made from corn, or maize, kernels used for thickening sauces and to add a transparent glaze to stir-fried dishes.

Cumin: the seed of the cumin plant, resembling caraway seeds, with a sweetish, mildly bitter and peppery taste. Available whole and powdered.

Curry pastes: spicy, fragrant pastes—red, green and yellow—used as the basic seasoning in many Thai dishes, including curries. Also available ready-made.

Curry powder: a mixture of dried, ground spices, such as turmeric, cayenne pepper, ginger, cumin, cinnamon and cloves, used for flavouring curries. Available commercially as a powder or a paste.

Durian: melon-sized fruit with a spiky skin, native to Southeast Asia. Though it has an unpleasant pungent smell when opened, the Thais consider its creamy, custard-like flesh to be delicious.

Fish sauce (*nam plah*): a thin brown sauce with a powerful aroma made from salted, fermented fish such as anchovies, used as a basic ingredient and salt substitute in Thai cuisine. Different makes of fish sauce vary in colour, flavour and strength, so you may need to adjust recommended amounts in these recipes, depending on the strength of the sauce.

Galangal (also called Thai ginger): a rhizome similar to ginger used for flavouring. *See also page 52.*

Garlic: an indispensable flavouring in Thai cuisine. Thai garlic is smaller and milder than its Western counterpart but may be difficult to find; if unavailable, substitute the ordinary variety.

Ginger root: the spicy, underground stem of the ginger plant, an important ingredient in Asian cuisine. Fresh ginger should be hard and wrinkle free. To store, put the ginger in an unwaxed paper bag, place this in a plastic bag and store in the refrigerator; it will keep for several weeks. Dried powdered ginger tastes very different and is not a suitable substitute.

Guava: fragrant, pear-shaped tropical fruit with a high vitamin C content. It can be eaten raw—sprinkled with a little lime or lemon juice—or stewed.

Glutinous rice: round-grained starchy rice, a staple in northern Thailand and used for sweet dishes throughout the country. *See also page 81.*

Kaffir lime (wild lime): a small, pear-shaped green citrus fruit, with a knobbly rind and not much juice. It is an important flavouring in Southeast Asian cuisine, where both its zest and aromatic green leaves are used. *See also page 58.*

Lemon grass: thick, fibrous stalks with a lemon flavour, used to flavour soups, pastes and stuffings. *See also page 58.*

Longan: sweet, juicy, grape-sized fruit similar to a lychee. Available canned.

Lychee (also spelt litchi): sweetly fragrant round or oval fruit, native to China and Southeast Asia and long cultivated in Thailand. The succulent white flesh with its single shiny brown seed is encased in a brittle red outer shell. Available fresh and in cans.

Mango: tropical fruit with a delicious, rich and sticky pulp and a large seed. Abundant in Thailand, it is eaten as a dessert, or underripe mango can be added to salads or combined with smoked meats and seafood.

Mangosteen: unrelated to the mango, this is a round, apple-size fruit with purplish-brown skin and snowy white flesh. It has an exquisite sweet-and-sour flavour. Best eaten just as it is.

Marinade: a seasoning mixture to coat or soak meat or fish before cooking in order to tenderize or impart flavour.

Mushrooms, dried Chinese: dried fungi used widely for their particular flavour and aroma. Sold in boxes or bags, they can be stored in airtight jars and must be soaked before use.

Oyster sauce: thick sauce blended from soy sauce, oyster extract and spices, used both in cooking meat and vegetables, and as a condiment.

Palm sugar: made from the sap of the palmyra palm, and yellowish brown in colour. It is less sweet than white sugar, with a slight caramel flavour, and can be bought in cans or blocks in Oriental food shops. If you cannot find palm sugar, Demerara or other soft brown sugar can be used instead.

Papaya (also called pawpaw): long pear-shaped tropical fruit with fragrant, peachy-coloured flesh and black seeds. *See also page 93.*

Peanuts: strictly speaking, not nuts but beans, which grow underground—hence their alternative name of groundnuts. Highly nutritious, they can be eaten raw or roasted and are used for making peanut butter and peanut oil. They are used in Southeast Asian and Indonesian cuisine in stews and sauces.

Peppercorns: the berries of the pepper vine *piper nigrum*. Originally native to India, it is the world's most-used spice. The fresh, unripe green peppercorns— sometimes available attached to their stalk—have a milder flavour than black peppercorns, which are the green berries fermented and dried. Fully ripe, the berries turn red; white peppercorns are the dried ripe berries that have been soaked and peeled.

Pimiento (also called Spanish pepper): a relative of the sweet pepper, but smaller and narrower in shape and much hotter in flavour. It is a good alternative to mild chilies. As for chilies, care should be taken when handling pimientos because of their volatile oils (*see Chilies*).

Pomelo: pear-shaped citrus fruit similar to grapefruit, but with a rather sweeter flavour and pinkish-yellow flesh.

Rambutan: small tropical fruit with a reddish skin covered in soft hairy spines. Its flesh and taste are similar to the lychee. Available fresh or canned.

Rice flour (also called rice powder): fine flour made from non-glutinous rice, used for thickening savoury dishes. Glutinous rice flour is made from glutinous rice.

Rice-paper wrappers: wrappers made from ground rice and used for wrapping round fillings, then frying. Available vacuum-packed or dry, they come in several sizes. Dry rice-paper wrappers are brittle and need to be moistened to make them pliable before use.

Rice vinegar: vinegar made from fermented rice wine used throughout Asia. There are different varieties of Chinese and Japanese rice vinegars, but Thais generally prefer it white. Rice vinegar contains less acid than wine vinegar, but if unavailable, smaller quantities of wine vinegar, or a milder variety such as Italian balsamic vinegar, can be substituted.

Rice wine: wine made from fermented glutinous rice. If unavailable, medium-dry sherry can be substituted.

Sesame oil: oil produced from roasted sesame seeds that has a nutty, smoky aroma; used mainly for seasoning.

Sesame seeds: tiny black or white seeds from the sesame plant used in sweet and savoury dishes, breads and pastries, as well as for making oil.

Shallots: a subtly-flavoured relative of the onion, used for flavouring or as a vegetable.

Shrimp paste or sauce (*gapi*): flavouring agent made from ground, fermented shrimps, and sold in jars. Good for seasoning vegetables, seafood and soups.

Soy sauce: savoury seasoning made from fermented soya beans, salt, wheat and yeast. Available in dark and light types, there is also a sweet soy sauce.

Spring roll wrappers: thin, white dough skins, between 15 and 25 cm square. Because they must be very thin, they are tricky to make at home, but are available frozen from Oriental food stores.

Steaming: to cook food in vapour from boiling water; one of the best techniques for preserving nutrients and flavours.

Stir-fry: Oriental cooking technique in which meat and vegetables are constantly stirred in a wok or frying pan, making them crisp but tender.

Sweet soy sauce: a sweet form of soy sauce, also called Javanese soy sauce or *ketchup manis*. *See also* Soy sauce.

Sweetcorns, baby: crisp, sweet miniature variety of sweetcorn, or maize, used in stir-fried dishes and salads. Baby sweetcorns are available fresh or frozen; the ones canned in vinegar are too sour.

Tamarind: the pods of the tamarind tree, from which a tangy flavouring is derived. *See also page 113.*

Tapioca flour: starchy flour, produced from various tropical roots, mainly from the manioc root.

Tempura flour: starchy flour, similar to potato flour. Mixed with water, it is used to thicken sauces and to make the famous tempura batter.

Thai fragrant rice: the most commonly used long-grained rice in Thailand. *See also page 81.*

Tofu (also called bean curd): a dense, mild soya bean product. Available in a soft, junket-like variety used in soups, or in firm cakes used for stir-frying, braising or poaching. Available fresh or vacuum-packed, tofu keeps refrigerated in water for up to 5 days. Drain well before using.

White radish (also called mooli or daikon): a long white root vegetable valued as a health food and used in salads or as a garnish.

Wok: classic Chinese cooking pan that, because of its rounded shape, ensures even heat when stir-frying. A heavy frying pan is a suitable alternative, but tossing food over high heat is easier in a wok because of its depth.

Wood ear mushrooms (also called cloud-ear mushrooms, tree ears or tree fungi): oddly-shaped fungi that grow on old tree trunks. They have little flavour and are used more for their crunchy texture and dark colour. Available dried.

CONVERSION CHART

These figures are not exact equivalents, but have been rounded up or down slightly to make measuring easier.

Weight Equivalents		Volume Equivalents	
Metric	Imperial	Metric	Imperial
15 g	½ oz	8 cl	3 fl oz
30 g	1 oz	12.5 cl	4 fl oz
60 g	2 oz	15 cl	¼ pint
90 g	3 oz	17.5 cl	6 fl oz
125 g	¼ lb	25 cl	8 fl oz
150 g	5 oz	30 cl	½ pint
200 g	7 oz	35 cl	12 fl oz
250 g	½ lb	45 cl	¾ pint
350 g	¾ lb	50 cl	16 fl oz
500 g	1 lb	60 cl	1 pint
1 kg	2 to 2¼ lb	1 litre	35 fl oz

TIME LIFE BOOKS

TIME-LIFE BOOKS

COOKERY AROUND THE WORLD
English edition staff for *Thailand*
Editorial: Ilse Gray, Luci Collings, Kate Cann
Production: Emma Wishart
Technical Consultant: Michael A. Barnes

English translation by Isabel Varea for Ros Schwartz Translations, London

Published originally under the title *Küchen der Welt: Thailand* by Gräfe und Unzer Verlag GmbH, Munich
© 1993 Gräfe und Unzer Verlag GmbH, Munich

This edition published by Time-Life Books B.V. Amsterdam
Authorized English language edition
© 1994 Time-Life Books B.V.
First English language printing 1994

TIME-LIFE is a trademark of Time Warner Inc. U.S.A.

ISBN 0 7054 1199 0

GRÄFE UND UNZER

EDITORS: Dr. Stephanie von Werz-Kovacs and Birgit Rademacker
Sub-Editor: Katharina Lisson
Designer: Konstantin Kern
Recipes tested by: Marianne Obermayr, Doris Leitner
Stylist: Duan Osbar
Production: BuchHaus.Kraxenberger.Gigler.GmbH
Cartography: Huber, Munich

Thidavadee Camsong, the author, was born in Thailand and studied marketing at Bangkok's Siam Commerce School, later working as a sales manager for a travel agency. She learnt classic Thai cuisine in her mother's restaurant. In 1989 she married a German, moved to Germany and now teaches Thai cookery at an adult education centre. She plays the *khim*, a traditional stringed instrument and represents Thailand at music festivals.

Foodphotography Eising Pete A. Eising and Susanne Eising specialize in food and drink photography and work closely with a food photographic agency operating in Germany and Switzerland. Their clients include publishers, advertising agencies and industrial companies. The food and props stylist responsible for this volume was Martina Görlach.

Heike Czygan, who did the illustrations for this book, is a designer working for a leading publishing house in Munich. While studying Sinology, she spent some time in China and became fascinated by ancient Oriental art styles.

Picture Credits

Colour illustrations: Heike Czygan

All photographs by Foodphotography Eising unless indicated below.

Cover: Graham Kirk, London. 4 (Unopened lotus blossoms, middle; Thai wedding, bottom right): Peter Lüffe, Bobingen. 4 (monks, Bangkok, top; Buddhas, Wat Mahathat, Bangkok, bottom, left), 5 (carved dragon, Wat Kukut, Lamphun, top; monk, Mat Hua Wang, middle; floating lotus flowers, below), 8-9 (floating vegetable market on Klong Damnoen Saduak), 10, 11 (2), 12: Martin Thomas, Aachen-Alt Lemiers. 13 top: Peter Lüffe, Bobingen. 13 bottom, 14 top: Martin Thomas, Aachen-Alt Lemiers. 14 bottom: Peter Lüffe, Bobingen. 15, 16: Martin Thomas, Aachen-Alt Lemiers. 17 top: T. Stankiewitz, Munich. 17 bottom, 18 (2), 19: Martin Thomas, Aachen-Alt Lemiers. 20 top: Hermann Rademacker, Munich. 20 middle and bottom: Peter Lüffe, Bobingen. 21 top: Bildagentur J Dziemballa, Munich:Lahr. 21 bottom: Hermann Rademacker, Munich. 22: T. Stankiewitz, Munich. 23 top: Martin Thomas, Aachen-Alt Lemiers. 23 bottom: Hermann Rademacker, Munich. 31, 33, 43: Martin Thomas, Aachen-Alt Lemiers. 47: Bildagentur Eising, Munich. 52: Peter Lüffe, Bobingen. 58: Martin Thomas, Aachen-Alt Lemiers. 71: Bildagentur Eising, Munich. 77: Peter Lüffe, Bobingen. 81, 93: Martin Thomas, Aachen-Alt Lemiers. 97: Peter Lüffe, Bobingen. 113: Bildagentur Eising, Munich. 135: Bildagentur J. Dziemballa, Munich:Imhof.

Colour reproduction by Fotolito Longo, Bolzano, Italy
Typeset by A. J. Latham Limited, Dunstable, Bedfordshire, England
Printed and bound by Mondadori, Verona, Italy

3 4 5 6 7 8 9 10 11 12 13 14 15 16 17 18 19 20 21 22 23 24 25 26 27 28 29 30